Renewal and the Middle Catholic

*"Who will give me to see before I die
the Church of God as in the good old days. . . ."*

St. Bernard of Clairvaux

Renewal
and the
Middle Catholic

William J. Bausch

FIDES PUBLISHERS, INC.
NOTRE DAME, INDIANA

© COPYRIGHT: 1971, FIDES PUBLISHERS, INC.
NOTRE DAME, INDIANA

NIHIL OBSTAT: LOUIS J. PUTZ, C.S.C.
UNIVERSITY OF NOTRE DAME

IMPRIMATUR: LEO A. PURSLEY, D.D.
BISHOP OF FORT WAYNE-SOUTH BEND

LCCCN: 71-129460
ISBN: 0-8190-0563-0

Contents

Introduction

Time magazine's Man and Woman of the year for 1969 were "The Middle Americans." They were those silent majority who cherish "a system of values that they see assaulted and mocked everywhere." Out-shouted and out-maneuvered by a liberal minority they have been, if not ignored then "treated with condescension." But at last, according to *Time*, they are beginning to assert themselves. They are responding with new displays of patriotism. They are lifting up their voices to be heard. They are expressing their political and social anguish. They are being recognized as a factor by politicians who were quick to perceive who put Richard Nixon into the White House.

It is not an unreal parallel to hold that, in the Catholic Church, there is a similar class of "Middle Americans," the "Middle Catholic." He (and she) is the one whose anguish is becoming more and more apparent. Like his political counter part he feels that for too long he has been out-shouted and out-maneuvered by religious liberals. He has indeed been treated with condescension as the vocal minority has gone ahead blithely defoliating his Mass, ridiculing his devotions, invading his parish, dismissing his morals and in general denigrating his One, Holy, Roman, Catholic Church.

The Middle Catholic feels that not only has he been betrayed by liberal laymen but also by liberal clergymen. Even the Pope has made too many concessions to both groups. In this climate, how does the Middle Catholic function? Can he function at all in the future? He thinks not as he sees more and more excesses, as he contemplates the permissive and frivolous youth of today.

The anguish of the Middle Catholic is real. He may be willing to concede that some things described by that overworked catch all word "renewal" have been an improvement; but renewal has gone too far. He is terribly threatened by it. He doesn't understand it. There are very few people to explain it to him either because renewal hasn't stopped long enough to be photographed and explained or the religious fads are proving to be so entertaining to the initiated that they haven't the time or inclination to explain renewal to others.

This book is ambitious because it seeks to take time out to talk to the Middle Catholic. It sweeps in a wide range from such topics as the liturgy, ecumenism, sex education and so on to a look at the good old days and an examination of the fear whether the Middle Catholic was really taught wrong in the past. It tries to explain the good points of renewal (there are some) as well as the faults. Read as a complete book it should give the Middle Catholic more facts to deal with, more of a position from which to assess present and future changes. The book leans strongly on the lessons of history in order to help the Middle Catholic see things in perspective today.

The extremes of the liberal-conservative labels will not like this book. Those who tend to be "ultra" in either camp will not be satisfied, but this book is not written for them. It is written for the average Middle Catholic who, while upset about renewal, is determined to keep an open mind.

Many of the thoughts, ideas and criticisms in this book are hardly original. They have come to the author from reading, but most of all from talking with the people, from listening to the Middle Catholic. The author himself is generally labeled as a "radical" or a "liberal" depending on the labeller. It should rejoice those who are fond of such labels to find so much latent conservatism. In any case, the author would prefer a book explaining and criticizing renewal for the Middle Catholic to be taken for what it is: a sincere effort to answer the needs of the people, to help them in difficult times to appreciate the firm presence of the Holy Spirit of God. The Middle Catholic himself who reads this book will alone testify whether the criterion has been met.

I wish to acknowledge the ideas of Frank Wessling of the Davenport (Iowa) Catholic Messenger on Catholic schools; those of Father Gerard Sloyan on liturgy; those of Father John Reedy and James F. Andrews on some points of renewal. I wish to acknowledge any ideas or thoughts that may have influenced me but whose names and sources are lost to memory. I wish to thank Ann DeVizia who so carefully untangled the manuscript and typed it for publication. Finally, I wish to thank all those Middle Catholics who spoke to me frankly and sincerely looking for help for their bewilderment, information for their minds and comfort for their souls—and who, by doing so, rendered me the same service.

CHAPTER I

The On-Going Liturgy . . .

— 1 —

It is only fitting that we should begin our look at Church renewal in wider perspective with the liturgy. The reasons are obvious. Disturbed as the average Catholic may be over protesting priests, picketing nuns and peculiar co-religionists these things, nevertheless, are off stage for him. They are in the wings creating noise and disturbance but not on center stage. But the Mass, *his* Mass, that's different.

"Be as kooky as you want but leave my Mass alone!" is the cry. And it's true. After all, the Mass is something that the good Catholic has attended every Sunday and holy day. He has grown into close familiarity with it. He has paid it the compliment of getting used to it. The Mass has meant a lot to him: its ceremonies, the lights and incense at high Mass, the Latin; in a word, the whole mystery of God among men. And now, now they—the leaders of the reform movement—have tried to strip the mystery away and lay bare its simplicity and something's been lost in the process.

It wasn't too bad, really, to have the priest facing the people. Many even have given grudging consent to the Mass in English, but guitars, dancing, banners—are these necessary? And the noise and bustle? The average, weary, commuting Catholic would like a little silence and rest at Mass instead of participation *every* minute and jumping up and down like jackrabbits and singing folk songs. Mass is so *busy* anymore!

There are the other shameful things we'd rather not think about. Underground churches and liturgies with their Bond bread rolls and Chianti wine. Way-out priests in T-shirts for vestments and dangerously suggestive kisses of peace. Readings from Ron McKuen and Charlie Brown. People taking communion in their own hands. What next?

No wonder that for the average Catholic his anger and frustration center around the liturgy. What in the world is going on? How did this ever come about. What's it all mean? Let's look. And when we say, "let's look" we mean let us look first at the Mass as we traditionally understand it, what the Mass really is and then we can see what the liturgists are trying to do with it.

The most profound and most obvious initial statement is that the Mass is the Christ-ed sacrifice. If we start off with this definition and explain it, the improvements and the mistakes of our present day liturgy will become clearer. The Mass as a sacrifice means that Jesus offered Himself totally to the heavenly Father. He surrendered everything; He held back nothing. He was the first representative of the human race to give so totally and by His total surrender we are saved. If we take the traditional four ends of Sacrifice—A-C-T-S—as we used to memorize them, we can see what happens when we take part in Mass.

"A". I come to church and I say, "My God, I adore you!" But in my heart I know that sentence is meaningless. "I adore *you?*" Would that I did! I really don't adore God, I adore myself. I serve myself like I am God. It's I, morning, noon and night. I adore, all right; I adore me in a million ways. I have made pride or money and the like my gods. How, then, can I really give proper adoration to the Father? The way I live belies the words. The words of adoration are empty, phoney, insincere. In short, *my* adoration is pathetic. But, something strikes me. Here I am trying to offer my adoration which I know is faulty. But Christ is here, my Leader, my Savior, the Perfect Adorer. He is speaking true and sincere adoration in this Mass to His heavenly Father because not only was His whole life one of adoration ("I always do the thing that pleases my Father") but He summed it up in the perfect and total giving of Himself on Calvary, which donation He left us in the Mass.

So, here's what I'll do at Mass. I'll grasp *His* adoration and offer *that* to God! That's what the Mass is about anyway: the mystery of Christ's givingness given to me. Here the Son is speaking true and sincere adoration and I will include mine in His so that, in His name and "with Him and through Him and in Him" I can worship the Father. You see, my adoration was empty and vain until I joined my noncommitted adoration to Christ's fully committed adoration. I "Christ-ed" my adoration at the Mass. I have sacrificed well to God the precise moment that the "I" blended into the "we" and the "we" included Christ; at the precise moment when Calvary's donation was made present to me at the Mass.

"C": contrition. I look down at my hands and see them crimson with evil and scarlet with sin. Well, maybe not so scarlet (at least that would indicate vigor) but appallingly pink, as Msgr. Knox once said, indicating that we didn't have enough gumption even to commit a major sin. But there we are, conscious of our evil and we are ashamed and appalled. Like Lady Macbeth we tell the spots of our sins to begone, but there they are. Miserable creatures that we are! What shall we do with these sins of ours? What operation shall pluck them from us, what surgery cut them out? What can we *say* before God to tell Him that we are sorry?

But, we recall one thing: in the Mass we have not only adequate apology, but the very statement of restoration, of healing, of renewal. That statement is Christ crucified and made present in the Mass. That statement is the sacrifice of Christ. If I say that I am sorry, it means nothing. If I utter a word of contrition, it says nothing. But if I and Christ, if *we* offer up that bleeding body and crowned head and crucified form, then *that* says "I'm sorry" like nothing else before or since in the world. The apology is a living and real thing. Christ becomes my perfect expression of contrition. Only because of Christ can my sinful lips speak sorrow. Only because of Christ can my crimes turn to contrition. Thus my contrition is "Christ-ed" in the Mass and therefore made perfect. In the Mass I have just said through Christ what I could not adequately speak myself.

The "T" for thanksgiving follows the same line of thought. In fact, thanksgiving is the very name we give to our Mass-action: the *Eucharist*. It implies all that we said above: a transferred utterance of gratitude through the lips of Christ, an utterance which not only includes gratitude for this very sacrifice of Christ but for the more simple and profound statement of fact spoken in the *Gloria,* "we thank you for your great glory." "Yes," we are saying, "just because You are You, we thank you eternally." Our word of thanksgiving is forever uttered through the Word at Mass.

The "S" stands for supplication. I supplicate. I ask God for the material and spiritual needs of my life. But there is an automatic flyer, as it were, to such supplications, a constant clause that's attached to all of my prayers; namely, I ask this *if this be Your will.* But, again, knowing myself as I do, I can't say and mean "Thy will be done!" I simply can't lay down in Gethsemane's dust and say, "nevertheless, not mine, but Thy will be done." I can't say that and mean it. It says too much. I can't bring myself to utter these words with full and complete sincerity when I ask for something. Imagine the change in my life if I really grabbed hold of God's will!

But, again, if I have trouble in making supplication by inferring "Thy will be done," *we* do not. My voice falters, but *our* voice—the voices of Jesus and I in the sacrifice of the Mass—our voice gives perfect prayer and perfect supplication with perfect sincerity and meaning and acceptance. I have "Christ-ed" my supplication.

Thus, in the Mass we have a Perfect Sacrifice, Christ, who is our Adoration, Contrition, Thanksgiving and Supplication. In the Mass, we open our mouths, but He speaks; we spread our arms but He raises them up. In the sacrifice of the Mass Jesus is our constant crucified Spokesman "ever making intercession for us" by uttering for us and with us the ACTS of humankind.

This is the Mass. We have taken time on this so that our examination will help us to see the benefits and the liabilities of the new liturgical changes.

—2—

On the benefit side, there should be said something at the outset for the notion of change itself. Change has, as a matter of fact, been a part of the liturgy since earliest times and therefore just to cry out with "It's always been like that" is not a valid criticism of the liturgical changes. In fact, according to Father Gerard Sloyan, there are four general categories in the history of the Mass. In the first centuries there was the rather simple and flexible Mass where Mass was held in a large house (remember, in the early centuries, it was persecution time). The bishop is there facing the people and talking to them and praying in their everyday language which happened to be Greek. He says a simple prayer of thanksgiving (*eucharistia*), all partake of communion and that's all. In this ancient form the Mass was thus simple with its prayer of thanksgiving, the consecration and communion. Not unlike the Last Supper. It was flexible enough that the bishop could make up various prayers as he went along and the people prayed and sang together and received communion under both species.

The second phase in the history of the Mass Father Sloyan calls the Long and Complicated Mass and this is the Mass around the fifth or sixth centuries held in some big cathedral (Christianity was now legal). The altar is still a simple table and the priest is still facing the people but everything is longer, grander and more solemn. There are added prayers for the living and the dead, ceremonies borrowed outright from the Byzantine court ceremonial, including what early Christianity rejected as heathen practices: the genuflections, bowing, kissing, incense and candles. The cult of the saints and the martyrs became prominent at this era.

The third phase is the Far Away and Silent era. This is around the 9th and 10th centuries and for the first time in almost a thousand years there is silence. No one is talking or singing in church anymore because no one really understands the Latin language anymore. The choir has taken over all of the singing parts and is now separated from the sanctuary and stuck way in the back of church. The latter has been decorated with a backdrop thus forcing the priest to face that backdrop with his back to the people. The people's speaking parts have been taken over by the altar boys. No one went to communion and so far removed did the people become from what was going on that in the 13th century the people clamored to at least see the Host and chalice and thus was introduced the elevation of the sacred species. When you recall how large the cathedrals were and that these were the days before the electric light and the public address system you can appreciate the physical and emotional distance between people and their Mass.

The fourth and final category, which persisted until Vatican II's decrees, was the Mass of the Rubrics. The Council of Trent, in a praiseworthy attempt to regulate many abuses in the Mass, put out strict rules governing the Mass and very minute rubrics concerning everything from the way one wore the maniple to what to do if the priest dropped the Host. Trent froze the Mass into a precise ritual passively watched by the people who said their private devotions in the pews.

This brief resume underlines our original point: that change has been a part of the Mass's history. People who claim, in reference to the Old Latin Mass, "But that's the way it always was" simply do not know their history.

So, obviously we're in phase five in our changing Mass. What about this century's approaches? What are they and what is their justification? Well, for one thing, there's an attempt to make the Mass once more a public celebration of all the people. If we go back and read our Scripture we see what activity and participation there were at the first Mass. Since Jesus and His Apostles were celebrating the Passover meal, there was food, conversation, ritual, prayers, blessings and singing by all. ("And after reciting a hymn, they went out to Mount Olivet." Matt 26:30)

Obviously the first Mass was not a passive kind of TV watching, as Trent inadvertantly made it later, but a matter of community participation. The ACTS of Christ's sacrifice were to be the acts of the People of God. The almost exclusive use of the plural in the Mass prayers in every century always meant to point up this fact. Therefore, the new approaches in our day to the Mass is to restore, not invent, the people's role, a role they had for almost a thousand years! Many of the new changes are geared to the social principle. Thus, the music which was once the people's is being given back to them. (Because we have been silent so long in church our Catholic singing is pretty terrible.) The prayers, once spoken by the people, are being given back to them.

Finally, the very "attitude" of isolation and privacy is being set aside as not really in keeping with the worship of God. After all we are there as a People of God, the New Israel. Jesus died for mankind and mankind as a corporate body must render to God what is His. The idea of many people individually worshiping without reference to the others is like the participants at a birthday party all going off into separate rooms to eat the birthday cake. There's something in the nature of a birthday celebration that demands participation and sociability. One can do private things privately, but a birthday party is by definition an open and public affair. So with the Mass. It is a public worship of God; it demands participation and sociability. Private devotions and private prayers can be done privately, but the Mass is, by definition, *liturgy,* that is, the *public* worship of God by the assembled community.

And, as we are apt to forget, not only our local community. The assembled people of God come from other cultures and other lands and when they assemble they must do so on *their* terms not ours. They must worship with the unique and fervent expressions of their own rich traditions. That such "different" communities should not or could not do so is to place an artificial barrier to the spirit of the Gospel and to the genuinely home-made utterance of their ACTS through Christ. In other words, liturgy, the public worship of God in Christ by the people of God, must be as local and cultural as human beings themselves. They should not be made to use utterances and gestures foreign to themselves. Perhaps this is why Mississippi sharecroppers haven't become Catholics. The Mass in Latin is too hard for them to understand; it's not their idiom. Besides it doesn't contain the Gospel preaching they're very fond of. Preaching the Gospel in Africa and Asia has been an uphill and often stupidly frustrating road because Western man insisted that Easterners worship in a Western way or that black people accept wholly the white man's religion. A brief excerpt from the Catholic historian Henri Daniel Rops in his volume *The Catholic Reformation* gives one of many sad mistakes in the liturgical life of the Church in regard to pagan peoples:

> If there was one country where missionaries had made the mistake of trying to impose the framework and methods of European Catholicism upon native converts, that country was India. . . . The Archbishopric of Goa, with its suffragan bishoprics of Meliapur and Cranganor (not to mention Macao in China), pre-

sented a handsome facade behind which there was little spiritual reality—dioceses administered on European lines, and more Portuguese than Hindu. In 1599,
however, Catholicism won a notable success: the
200,000 descendants of the "Christians of St. Thomas"
in the region of Cochin, who were subject to the heret-
ical and schismatic Jacobite patriarch of Mesopotamia,
but who retained vivid memories of a visit paid to them
by St. Francis Xavier, determined to submit to the
Holy See. Unfortunately, they were soon led to regret
their decision by the stupidity of a few Western mis-
sionaries who wished forcibly to latinize the age-old
Syro-Chaldaic, and to forbid them to pray in the popular tongue of Malabar. The resulting tension produced a new schism of 1633 (pp: 292-293).

The historian also notes in the same volume the great
success of the great missionary Fr. de Nobili who suc-
ceeded precisely because he adopted the customs of
India, wore their clothes and lived among the people as
one of them. He studied their religions, found much
common tradition in them, let the natives retain their
customs and practices which were not unchristian—and
for this he was called before the Inquisition at Goa! This
was the man who, when he died in 1656, left prosperous
missions with 100,000 Christians in various parts of
India. The point, again, is that the Mass is for all peoples and need not necessarily be tied down to one form
of liturgical expression. Another great missionary, St.
Paul, had the same approach:

> Even if I preach the Gospel, I can claim no credit for
> it; I cannot help myself; it would be misery for me not
> to preach. . . . I am a free man and own no master; but
> I have made myself every man's servant, to win over as
> many as possible. To Jews I became like a Jew to win
> Jews. . . . To win Gentiles who are outside the Law, I
> made myself like one of them. . . . To the weak I be-

came weak to win the weak. Indeed I have become everything in turn to men of every sort, so that in one way or another I may save some. All this I do for the sake of the Gospel, to bear my part in proclaiming it (1 Cor 16-23).

It took a long time, but we have learned from such experiences as this. Now any People of God assembled for their worship in Christ may do so with their own unique genius as is evident by the wide variety of liturgies now permitted (even with the local communities) and the use of the vernacular.

Thus participation, maneuverability and change in the Mass and indeed in many other liturgical matters, are a matter of history and of need. The truth can be expressed in many ways. The problem of today, as seen by some, is that the Mass, as it used to be simply became so passive, so "mysterious" and so distant that it became unreal and meaningless for many people except as a background to fulfill their obligation and say their prayers. The Mass became out of harmony with its own inner nature as community worship. It was a long way from the original intimate Passover of the first Mass with its love-talk, Scripture and song-singing by all to the passive silent presence of the people in the pew lulled by the sound of an unknown language. Too many accretions had gathered in the liturgy which no longer carried meaning to the industrialized person, much less the space age person.

Still less did it build community for him. The decree on the Liturgy was thus right in proclaiming, "These [old forms] not only may but ought to be changed with the passage of time if they have suffered from the intrusion of anything out of harmony with the inner nature of the liturgy or have become unsuited to it" (art. 21).

And in the new decree on the new changes in the Mass issued by Paul VI for March 22, 1970 (in the United States), the Holy Father made explicit reference to the antiquity of changes and the centuries-old preparation for them.

> No one should think, however, that this revision of the Roman Missal has been suddenly accomplished. The progress of liturgical science in the last four centuries has certainly prepared the way. After the Council of Trent, the study "of ancient manuscripts in the Vatican library and elsewhere," as Saint Pius V indicated in the apostolic constitution *Quo primum,* helped greatly in the correction of the Roman Missal. Since then, however, other ancient sources have been discovered and published, and liturgical formulas of the Eastern Church have been studied. Many wish that these doctrinal and spiritual riches not be hidden in libraries, but be brought to the light to illumine and nourish the minds and spirits of Christians. (Apostolic Constitution, April 3, 1969)

If we accept the historical fact of change in the Mass over the centuries and the necessity of the public expression of the ACTS of Christ by the assembled participants, then current change is the only alternative. Specific changes may be challenged and the manner in which they were made, but generally the changes have both incorporated ancient elements (as Pope Paul said) and are geared to make the Mass liturgy more meaningful. As such the changes have generally been helpful, have promoted a new appreciation of the Mass, have engaged more people actively in their assembled worship of God and have built up a spirit of community.

But not for all.

CHAPTER II

... And On

1

Not all have been happy with the changes in the Mass—which is perhaps the greatest understatement so far of the 1970's. In the January 1970 issue of the Catholic conservative magazine *Triumph* Jane Bret sums up the conservatist's feelings,

> The Catholic faithful are running away from a runaway liturgy. Yet the smaller the congregations and more disgruntled they become, the more an intellectually impoverished clergy strain to drum up one more burst of manufactured "meaning" to further activate a people already limp from meaning-run-wild.

> Almost any Mass one attends today is a case in point. We are herded like goats, read at, talked at, sung at, preached at. Before the service begins there may be an impromptu choir practice. Then we may be put through a pre-Mass rehearsal to cultivate the proper mood. Whereupon the celebrant, with a few emotional phrases, tries to get us even more securely into the correct psychological posture for receiving all the meaning that is momentarily to come crashing down on us— or come surging out of us; much like the Old Faithful geyser at Yellowstone, right on schedule at twenty minutes past the hour.

> Liturgical robber-barons have simply stolen from under an unsuspecting and now suffering laity two thousand years of tradition, beauty, form, mystery and blessed silence. . . . .

In media language, the liturgical crusaders have liberated us *from* in order to shackle us to, literally drown us in *content*. All this is done, of course, in the name of participation. . . (and) participation feed-in can rapidly become an out-put of measurable enthusiasms. (A decision to join a picket line is an acceptable out-put— or anything else that will satisfy the scientific passion for showing that the Mass has *done* something) . . . .

The reformers' false emphasis on meaning has produced what media men call the "hot-test" of liturgy. Meaning is sought so strenuously that it is precisely the coveted meaning which is lost almost entirely. We so totally *know* what we are doing at Mass, whether turning pages or jumping up and down, that we lose the power to be carried away, to reach the immolated God Who Is. . . .

If Miss Bret doesn't have an exact sense of history ("two thousand years of tradition, beauty, form, mystery and blessed silence" have, as we have seen, not always been the order of the day anymore than candles, incense and handkissing), still she raises some interesting points. Let's offer some criticism in line with her thinking:

1. *The Mass today is too busy.* Perhaps it is, with all that singing and marching and up-and-downing and rehearsals. There is possibly a preoccupation at Mass today which prevents inner growth. This is why the new General Instruction and the New Order of the Mass, effective March 22, 1970 in the United States does provide for periods of silence.

2. *Some of the changes today, at least the experimental ones, are too tied to present day culture.* This is a more devastating criticism. With the guitars and folk songs and other multi-media apparatus, not to mention dancing nuns doing their thing, the Mass takes on the

aspect of a circus for some. Actually there is something to be said for giving *any* contemporary expression to God, for all demonstrations and all human celebrations of life, like Zorba's dance, are fit to lift up before Him. The only problem might be that such local and immediate expressions tend to be as ephemeral as the current best-selling rock song and give the appearance of instability and frivolity. Moreover, sometimes those who insist that the Church must be with it, "it" being present day culture, are often intolerant of another culture from the past. The last national liturgical conference was a horror to many enthusiasts who attended it. It was an experiment in multi-media happenings that caused many to wonder where the Mass came in. As a matter of fact, according to Rev. Joseph Connolly its president, the National Liturgical Conference has been cancelled for 1970 due to financial trouble and lack of interest. If the changes are too tied down to current culture, they will be as obsolete as last year's popular singer.

3. *The mystery of Mass is being bared to the point of extinction.* With everything so explained and so dissected, there may be no room for the transcendental. A kind of scientism has invaded the sanctuary. Mystery cannot be explained; it should be pointed up and framed for contemplation. But contemplation is "out" today and the microscope on the altar has perhaps lessened the awe and reverence that should pervade any encounter with the Almighty.

4. *A serious criticism of the new liturgies is that they are guilty of an overemphasis on the community.* Yes, the People of God are surrounding the eucharistic table. The meal aspect becomes very important. Holding hands at the Our Father, giving the kiss of peace and going out and doing something overt with one's Mass

are urgent priorities in today's liturgy, the center of the Christian life. But Daniel Callahan, no conservative, upset the liturgical backers when he challenged the liturgists to prove this. He had the boldness to question whether the liturgy really *is* "the center and source of the Christian life" as the Decree of the Liturgy proclaimed. He sees no evidence that the new liturgy is causing a measurable renewal among Christians. In fact, Callahan maintains that the liturgy is *not* the center of the Christian life and that a preoccupation with the liturgy is a defense which gives the idea that Christ *can* be caught in the eucharistic mystery so why seek Him among men? The liturgy does not, he maintains, build up community; in fact, one needs community first to build up the liturgy. In the September 9, 1967 issue of *Ave Maria,* James Andrews editorialized on Callahan's position:

> In retrospect, some feel that a few serious mistakes have been made. The Liturgical Conference became strong because of the obvious urgency of its cause. It attracted thousands who were appalled at the liturgy of the preconciliar Church. When aggiornamento was not even a coined word, the conference sought renewal and patiently carried out the scholarship and discussion so essential. The best theologians, the most progressive pastors, the enthusiastic seminarians and sisters, all gravitated to the conference. There did seem to be a subconscious and actually often expressed presumption, as Callahan claims, that the reform of the liturgy was the key to Christian renewal—to parish renewal.

> But now, according to many pastors at the conference, the true, sober reality is surfacing. The massive conference is a tail wagging the dog. In other words, we have made the mistake of thinking that parish renewal

means liturgical renewal. We have thought that the answer to our lifeless parish life was the revitalization of the liturgy. We have been profoundly wrong.

Father William F. Nerin, pastor of the famed experimental parish called the "Community of John XXIII" in Oklahoma City—the first officially authorized parish without geographical boundaries or a building of its own—says that the Catholic Church has been wasting its time and energy on the theory that the Eucharist "creates and builds community." This does not stand the test of pastoral experience.

According to Father Nerin, if the parish is to be alive and "renewed" it must hold common purposes and goals which center primarily around the concerns of man outside of the community (parish) in terms of being a servant of that man in the secular world.

This last point brings up what some call the second mistake made by the Liturgical Conference: the emphasis on education. If one keeps in mind the first problem (we have equated parish renewal with liturgical renewal) it is clear that a massive educational assault—with a heart of liturgical theology—could easily become the focus of parish activity. In fact, in many parishes, this is exactly what has happened.

The point is that community cannot be built in a vacuum—even with the help of films, lights and handclapping—and to answer this objection by referring to faith is to rely on an incomplete theology. For it is basically true that what happens at Mass in the way of building community happens in proportion to what the community brings. . . .

5. *The new liturgy has not replaced traditional symbols.* Too often traditional pictures, statues, gestures, music (for example, Gregorian chant) and the like have been deleted and nothing universal put in their places. One may dismiss these old culture symbols

as superstition or folk religion but this is to overlook the fact that no community can exist without customs and symbols that in themselves might be irrational but which, nevertheless, bind the community together. The old lady moving her lips before an old-world Madonna might elicit a smile from the young intellectual, but even he had no doubt either about the faith in her heart or the ultimate theological reality which underlay a devotion gone astray.

One wishes that the reformers of the liturgy had made more effort to renew and re-inform (in the old scholastic sense) the symbols before dismissing them or ridiculing them into disappearance. After all, Catholics, like all other groups from the Kiwanis to Fred Flintstone's Loyal Order of Buffalo, do not or did not so much take meaning from the old liturgy and its symbols as bring meaning to them. True some symbols became parasitical and tended to choke off more valuable and more genuine liturgical realities, but again a renewal of the symbols was more in order than letting them go altogether. As a result there seems to be few universal symbols to bind the Catholic community together today. Nor, it might be added, are the worded banners or any other "linear" approach much of a substitute as they tend to be too local. In fact, if McLuhan is right, they are not effective either in a world retreating from the written word to high ritual and audio-visual symbol— witness the ritual clothes, rock music, peace symbols and drug culture which bind the global youth community together.

6. *Finally, fellowship has overshadowed sacrifice.* As we saw at the beginning, the Mass is a sacrifice; it is the whole Christ uttering the ACTS to the Father; it is Calvary, that apex of total donation and complete sur-

render. The purpose of Calvary, of course, is not only unspeakable worship but to help men to love one another. That is why there was so much love-talk at the Last Supper. Thus fraternity and loving one's neighbors whom one sees is important and even critical if the sacrifice is to mean something at all to man. But there is the danger of this product overshadowing the Person, the result outshining the Cause, the fraternity replacing the Fatherhood. At Mass we are indeed brothers, but brothers by adoption. It is Christ's holiness that flows from the divinity into His humanity into us who are mystically joined with and to Him (Marmion). It is Christ's surrender that is the unity and hope of all men. The Mass is a sacrifice not merely an occasion for fraternity. Indeed, the effect of the sacrifice should make us more fraternal but only so we can worship God together. The slant seems to have shifted from heaven to earth. So much emphasis on ecclesiastical togetherness and what amounts to a kind of sacramental sensitivity session at Mass tends to subvert He Who Is and cause us not to notice Him who is "always living to make intercession for us." It is the crucified Christ Who makes our ACTS His and His ours.

Perhaps the case on the liturgy was best summed up by that profound and magnificent layman, Frank Sheed when he wrote in *Spectrum of Catholic Attitude:*

> In heaven Christ continues His offering of himself, once slain on Calvary, now forever living, to his heavenly Father—for the application to men of the Redemption he won for the race (Heb 7: 24-5).

> The Mass is the breaking through to our altars of this intercession—the priest, in the name and in the power of Christ, offers the same Christ—once slain, now forever living—to the same Heavenly Father for the same

purpose. We of the laity are lifted into the splendor of this action—"my sacrifice and yours," says the priest. Compared with what Christ and the priest and we are joined in doing, details of vestments or street clothes, church or somebody's kitchen table, ancient language or vernacular are secondary—not unimportant, but not primary. They will be good or less good according as they express the mind and heart of the worshippers. The danger is, of course, that the liturgical experts may take over: and they are more likely than not to be out of touch with the mind and heart of the rest of us. If we all come to a living awareness of what is being done at the altar and of our part in it, there will be a change in the congregation which will do more than any number of changes in rituals (p. 147).

Still, these are criticisms that do not touch the desirability of change itself. They only comment on the possible results and manner of some of the changes. The Church is an on-going Church and its people a people of current expression, aspirations and hopes. They are a People of God and Brothers in Christ; they are a "royal priesthood." As such, worship is their nature and Christian worship their right. In performing their ACTS in Christ Jesus, they are entitled to all that an assembled people can do to make those ACTS meaningful, social and fraternal. For a thousand years they did have meaningful participation. It is a blessing of our age that this right and privilege is being restored. Arguments can be raised about the ways and means of liturgical changes. None can be raised about the need for changes now nor (as we have shown) their existence in history then.

— 2 —

When my father died we were all very sad. We had the funeral viewing in our home. Since my father was well known and well loved in town, we had a large crowd coming in and out every night. Everyone, of course, had a few words of consolation to say to my grieving mother. My brothers and sisters stood there as a kind of reception line to speak to the people and be near our mother. In short, we were following the strict protocol of funeral viewing and everyone was conforming. All of a sudden, Mrs. Juliano who rented one of our apartments came in. She said a prayer at the coffin, went over to my mother and in full stage whisper said, "Here's your rent money!" Well, we all burst out laughing. It certainly wasn't the most appropriate thing to say nor the most solemn sentiment. Mrs. Juliano probably felt, however, that this might make my mother happy and she gave what comfort she thought that any landlady would like to receive. And in her own way and from her undeniable charity, she was right.

This points up the fact that there will always be a difference between group protocol on a given occasion and personal expression. So, maybe she wasn't in line with the others. So maybe her rent money was not the most apt sign at the moment. But it was her approach and represented her thoughtfulness and what more can one say? In the liturgy it is the same. There is something in the very nature of the liturgy that demands apt protocol. If the liturgy is the community's offering to God of the sacrifice of Christ, then, somehow, the ceremonies ought to express that.

Perhaps the biggest fight today between those for and against the new liturgy is one of opinion: does the new way really express what the liturgy is all about? Its proponents say yes and to that end changes have been made: more participation, a fuller voice at the Mass and so on. Yet, there's something to be said for the Mrs. Julianos of the world. Maybe at the liturgy she wants to say the novena to St. Jude. Granted, that's a private devotion and not really apt at the public gathering—she should say private things privately—but there should be room for her. She should be able to go to God and say the prayerful equivalent of "Here's your rent money!" There have been cases of boorish priests who have denounced the Rosary-saying members of the congregation. There have been instances where crude and rude clergy have told the people to stay home if they can't sing out in church. There's no reason here to defend the indefensible. Discourtesy is not confined to the layman. No, there should be room in the Church for the personal expression of people who want to spell love in a different language.

We haven't said much about those liturgical eccentricities referred to at the beginning of the first chapter such as some priests grabbing the Wonder bread off the table and consecrating it, or Masses said with hot dog rolls in T shirts and Bermuda shorts. There are instances where, after the homily is over (usually a comment on a Beatle song) the priest and people smoke marijuana to help the mystic-feeling grow. There's nothing to say about these far out affairs except that they represent abberations and the juvenile reactions of some who don't really know what the Mass is all about. But the greater harm is the bad name they give to genuine experimentation and bona fide expressions of the Church's desire to renew the liturgy for, if some of these experimentations do take on the appearance of eccentricities to the average Catholic, it should be remembered that there is nothing wrong in experimentation itself. The Mass belongs to the people and ways and means must be considered which will make the Christ-among-us more meaningful. It is often the people themselves and their local pastors who will hit on genuine and authentic ways of worshiping and so the search must go on. It's just that extremist liturgies are just that: extremist. They do not necessarily represent the best of the new liturgy or liturgical experimentation. They do not necessarily express the genuine steps being made in the constant evolution of man's approach to God through Christ in the great mystery of the Mass.

— 3 —

Let us conclude with some present and future changes outside of the Mass that the average Catholic will run into which will likely have startling or surprising effects. First of all, as is being done in some places already, the next time he goes to a funeral he may see the vestments in white, the music with alleluias printed throughout and the prayers in terms, not of death, but of resurrection. The wry thought that passes through his mind that somehow "we're glad you're gone, you rascal, you" must be resisted. Rather what we have here is no change of doctrine, but a fine example of the *same doctrine with a different emphasis*. Formerly, we stressed the mournful aspects of death: the music was somber, the trappings black and the prayers intercessory. Spoken of were the "depths," the sinfulness of the deceased, especially those sins committed in the passion of youth, the plea that the deceased may not undergo the pains of hell. There is nothing wrong here and the mood could be as touching as the beautiful *"Dies Irae"* could be sublime.

But this was a reflection of a former era when men over-stressed the Passion of Christ and left in the shadow the main event for which the Passion prepared:

the Resurrection. The Resurrection has always been the central doctrine and the central liturgy of the Church, old and new. Through a misemphasis on one point of sin and death, the glory of the Resurrection has receded into the background. The new funeral liturgy brings the Resurrection out of the background and into the light. We *do* believe in a life after death. Jesus has conquered death and made our resurrection possible. We *do* believe that death is the door and, as such, a truly happy event for a person to go back to God. As did the early Christians, we should rejoice. We should not rest our eyes entirely on the corpse, but we should lift them up to the resurrected person in the bosom of the Father. So, why not the color white, the color of joy? Why not the alleluia, the resurrection song? Why not Christian joy among the human sorrow?

When the mother of Monsignor Fox—that great priest who has worked so hard with the poor and under-privileged in New York—died the holy card printed for her read:

> to celebrate
> Margaret M. Fox
> who came to the
> fullness of her life on
> November 9, 1969
>
> Lord, we thank you
> for the life of
> Margaret Fox
> who walked in gentleness
> and spent herself
> in making peace
> We trust that as
> she chose you in life
> you will now choose
> her for life eternal
> amen.

"She came to the fullness of her life." Indeed, this is a Christian proclamation, not of the death she died on November 9, 1969, but on the new life she entered in Christ on that day.

In the same vein, Catholics will begin to notice the appearance of a Fifteenth Station and it will be "The Resurrection." The emphasis, of course, will be the same: the crucifixion and burial are but steps to the final victory. The Resurrection is the central reality and alone gives any sense to life and death. To include it among the fourteen stations is to bring back into focus this truth.

The size, shape and substance of the communion host is changing and will change dramatically. Again, not in essence, but in an importantly incidental way (if that isn't a contradiction). The hosts received by the people and used by the priest at Mass will be more "meaty," more substantial. They will be whole wheat and/or they will be hearty so that genuine chewing will be required. Once more there is here a matter of emphasis. The eucharistic doctrine is the same, the point to be given priority is heightened. Jesus did say at the Last Supper, "take and eat." He used the Jewish unleavened bread which was hardly the white, paper-thin host we know today. It was bread-y and it was capable of being grabbed and broken. Sometimes those white hosts are so thin one can't even chew them. In fact, older Catholics will remember that it was wrong to chew the host because someone piously (but erroneously) thought that one's teeth could somehow damage Jesus. The change to larger, more substantial hosts is a change of emphasis that the Mass has a meal aspect, that real bread-breaking and real bread-sharing are a part of it. Some hosts may become so substantial that they may be too big for the priest to manage to place on the recipient's tongue. Thus the recipient will have to take the host-bread in his hand and give it to himself. This is not so startling when one remembers that in the early Church, the priest would give the left-over hosts to babies and small children in their mother's arms. Older Catholics must remember the inspiring story of Tarcisius, the boy who brought Holy Communion to the prisioners in jail. Only a boy, he carried the host and gave out Communion.

Communal confessions also represent a matter of emphasis. The former way of going to confession is still good and will always be. Communal confessions are merely private confessions in a public setting. The stress is on the community aspect of sin; that we not only offend Christ with our sins, but the Whole Christ, that is, all the members of His Mystical Body. Sin is social by nature; so, too, must be repentance.

There are more similar things coming in the liturgy just as there are more cherished traditions being dropped such as the blessing of the throats in some areas or blessing of the candles. It is not that these things are no longer good or valid. It is that someone wishes to place the emphasis elsewhere and by clearing the "distractions" of candles and ashes, etc. out of the way, a better perspective can be established. This is not to say that it is a good policy to do these things, but only to say that, as a matter of fact, a point of view plays a terribly important part in all of these things.

Speaking of a point of view, let us end our look at the liturgy with a comment that is very true for the average Catholic upset by the changes. The comment is, I believe, quite valid and it says that most problems about the liturgy are not really problems of dogma or doctrine (although in some cases it borders on that), but our problems are rooted in the emotional. By that I mean that all of the other ways, the black funeral Mass, the rosary at the wake, the fourteen stations, the intimacy of the private confession—all of these things are more than cherished devotions to many people. They are highly overlaid with emotional overtones. It's the whole "atmosphere" of security and happy memories that are attached to many of these things, and that's why we are reluctant to let them go. It's not unlike the truism that no wife can cook like Mom. As a matter of objective fact, the wife may be a far better cook, but the husband doesn't feel so. Actually, when he looks back in fond memory on his mother's cookery, it's not the food itself nor her culinary art that was really important, but a whole overtone of fussing and caring and cajoling that mattered. It was not the food, it was the large serving of love that made Mom's dinner so pleasing. So it is with so many of the changes which disturb people in the liturgy. It's really not the changes, as much as that large serving of familiarity, comfort and security that they miss. For this, they cannot be faulted. Their only obligation in all of the liturgical changes is to keep an open mind and try to bring to the new ways some of the peace and security they found in the old.

CHAPTER III

The Changing Parish

– 1 –

Just as the changes in the liturgy have affected and even puzzled the Middle Catholic because of the nearness and dearness of his Mass, so too have the changes taking place in his parish. Outside of the lack of the old time devotions (which we'll speak about below) and perhaps a few folk Masses, the parish may look the same on the outside but inwardly, structurally, it is changing too. For one thing, the layman is moving in. True, he's already moved into the sanctuary. The average Catholic is getting used to seeing him standing at the lectern leading the prayers or the singing. The average Catholic has even seen the layman take part in the Offertory procession in some parishes. That's not what is meant. What is meant is that the parish is changing radically in that the layman is beginning to share responsibility for the very running of the parish. He is being joined by others to form boards known in most places as Parish Councils. A Parish Council assists the pastor in the administration and policies of the parish. To many older Catholics this may seem like a come-down for the pastor. After all, the pastor has run the parish all these years without laymen butting in and telling him how to do his work. Why, all of a sudden, is the pastor seemingly inadequate to do his job now? Why this scramble of the layman to enter areas in which he really doesn't belong? Who is *really* running the parish?

To understand the shift from the one man pastoral "boss" to the more democratic council arrangement, it is necessary (as it is so often in the course of our investigations) to move back into history and see the parish in perspective.

Try to visualize the symbol of the old time American parish as that of a pyramid composed of eight layers. The lowest, bottom layer would be labeled "Ethnic-Immigrant." This refers to the historical fact that most American Catholics are first or second generation since our parents and grandparents came over from the other side. When they came they found that they, as foreignors, were in alien territories and gave these territories their own peculiar tone. In fact, they often duplicated as much as they could of the old country. The testimony to this is that even to this day ethnic islands called "Little Italy" or "Little Poland" dot our big cities.

For the average old world immigrants, the Church was a most essential and intimate part of their lives and thus they also imported that church as a part of their customs and heritage. They brought their own priests, they maintained their old practices and they rallied around their Mass and sacraments. The priest especially had great importance for them. Not only was he a symbol of continuity from the old country but he was an able interpreter of the new. Often he was the only one who could speak some English, the only one sufficiently educated to lead the way. The imported pastor performed a noble service in the acclimation of his people to the new world.

The second layer of this symbolic parish pyramid might be labeled "language." Unless the immigrants were from England or Ireland, they spoke a "foreign" tongue in the new country. They were an alien voice and this tended to draw them closer together. Naturally, they held on to their own language in their parishes and had services in their native tongue.

But being foreign-speaking immigrants wasn't the only area of adjustment. There were others. For one thing the immigrants found that they had moved into a "Protestant" country. These Protestants resented those foreign immigrants and bigotry against Catholics (as we'll see in another chapter) was a favorite indoor sport. The historian Arthur Schlesinger, Sr., has remarked that the blackest page in American history is the prejudice against Catholics. The anti-Catholics formed into Know-Nothing and APA groups and POAU organizations. Signs at employment agencies read, "Dogs and Irish need not apply." Protestants so took over the public school system and so taught anti-Catholicism that the Catholics responded with the introduction of their own parochial school system. This sort of thing constituted the dynamics of the third layer in the old time parish pyramid, "Defensism." Catholics had to defend themselves against the Protestants. This stance tended to make them huddle more closely together around their church, its service and their pastor who might well be the most formidable and most staunch anti-Protestant. The pastor symbolized both defiance and resistance. Through him the "true" religion was preached.

The next layer in the pyramid is called "Isolation," an understandable outcome of all that has been said so far. Catholics, like the Jews, tended to ghettoize for protection. Safe in their own areas, staying close to the church, they did not always fit into the mainstream of community life and indeed were not always welcome. They often preferred to stay in their own communities. There was security among their own and their own especially included their pastor.

A fifth layer was what we shall call "poverty." Most immigrants came to the country to work. And work they did. They were pulled quickly into the new industrial factory system. They worked long hours and their children, before social legislation, worked in the sweat shops. The average immigrant was poor, working his way on up. Being poor and his energies going into economic adjustment and survival he did not have time for other sociabilities beyond those of his ghetto and beyond those promoted by his church. True, some Catholic laymen had a brief and stormy fling at trusteeism—calling, appointing and dismissing their pastors much to the chagrin of the bishops—but even this was more nationalistic than ecclesiastical, more a reflection of the tightness of the pyramid than a going beyond it. No, active parish participation was confined to passivity or joining the anti-Masonic Knights of Columbus or such. To be any part of the parish's administration was not even thought of even if there were the leisure and financial stability to be so.

The next two layers of the pyramid are interrelated. The one is labeled "education." Very few immigrants were educated nor was it really necessary that they should be. Schooling was kept at a minimum. Work was primary and society did not demand higher education for its citizens. This was but a reflection of the other layer, the "simple life." Although the industrial revolution had dawned, the technological revolution had not. Life was still pretty simple. There was work, play and church-going in well defined patterns. Birth, death and marriage were precise affairs. No knowledge explosion was even thought of, speed was too new to cause attention, the airplane was in its infancy and the automobile was exciting but localized. In parish life this was translated into the fact that the competent well educated pastor could run the parish without too much complication.

Finally, at the top, that is, the top layer of the parish pyramid, stood the pastor himself. Sometimes he was there as symbolic of great authority, a reassuring figure from the old world, dispensing the graces of God and keeping morals in order. But he was a reassuring figure for the new world as well. He was a real Father to his people, aiding in their Americanization, helping them to adjust in the new country and being their local mayor, lawyer, doctor and priest. He was self-assured, competent, free to be master of the parish domain and able to control the well defined pyramid system.

This, then, is the description of the old time parish structure. A tight knit pyramid, a stabilizing influence, a fortress in a foreign land. The question is, is this symbol valid today? Times have changed is a cliche, but often we do not realize how much. But to see how much, let us briefly counterpoint the layers of the pyramid.

At the bottom, we no longer have the "ethnic-immigrant" base. The simple fact is that we are all first or second or third generation Americans. We have melted into the melting pot of this nation. "Little Italy" and "Little Poland" may be quaint today, but they are anachronisms and are no longer places of refuge. This is also true of the parishes which served them and symbolized them. Language is no longer a barrier, so that this layer is not real anymore. We all speak English. Our "defensism" against the Protestants has officially disappeared. True, there is still prejudice around. True, we witnessed its blatant form in the campaigns of Alfred E. Smith and John F. Kennedy; but it was the latter who, together with that other John in the Vatican, gave the death blow to official prejudice. In fact, Catholics are now "in" and political campaigns in recent times find it politic to have a Catholic on the campaign slate.

The lowering of the prejudice barriers has been given impetus by the ecumenical activities of the churches. Officially, neither Protestants nor Catholics have to fight the Reformation anymore. Obviously, also, the layer we called "isolation" is no longer an important one. With official prejudice gone and a common language Catholics are well integrated into society today. They are a genuine part of the community in all of its aspects. Nor for the average American Catholic is poverty an all engrossing state of life. He is rather moderately wealthy. His working hours are well defined and in fact give him more time for education and leisure. Like his conferees in America today's Catholic takes advantage of his education and gets as much as he can. He does this not only because of the availability of higher education, but also, in today's society, it is a necessity. No longer is life simple (and thus another layer is invalid). It is terribly complex. The new technological society demands more education, more rules, more refinements, more specializations, and more dependency on the highly trained technician.

What we have tried to show is that, for the average Catholic, the symbol of his parish, the symbol of the pyramid, is not workable anymore. The "layers" have been changed or modified. The results for the parish structure should be obvious. First of all, the parish is an

integrated part of the community and no longer a fortress against it. It exists in an interrelating pattern of
many other systems, corporations and buildings. It is
one of many voices in the community. It is part of technology when it air conditions the church, part of public
interest when it busses children to its schools, part of the
government when it pays its withholding taxes for its
employees, part of the mass media when it introduces
closed circuit television into the classrooms.

Obviously, in this framework, the pastor's role must
change. He is no longer needed as old country symbol:
he too is an American. He is no longer needed as interpreter either of language or culture. He is no longer the
only educated man in town. In fact, he is well aware
that in his congregations there are people more educated than himself. If the church microphone breaks
down he must call in some technician to fix it. He needs
a lawyer to guide him in church legal affairs, a public
accountant to make out the tax reports, a mechanic to
fix his car and the repair man to mend his television. In
other words, in today's society the pastor is no longer
the President of the Corporation (although many still
perceive of themselves that way and are consequently
having the hardest time adjusting) but rather a leader
of the people. In fact, to return to our use of the symbol,
the pyramid structure of the parish has given way to the
circle structure. The pastor is now in the middle surrounded by his equals in their own fields working together for the building up of the Church. Today's society is too complex to have it otherwise. This, then, is
the reason for the introduction of Parish Councils.

The layman is moving into the parish administration
simply because he is needed. Parish life is too technical
and too complex for one man to oversee. A Parish Coun-

cil as a representative group of people, must advise the pastor in parish affairs. This arrangement received additional strength from the fact that many parishes are so huge that no one man can get to know the needs of everyone in his parish; representatives from the various parish areas can "tune in" the pastor. Moreover, with a Parish Council of laymen, the pastor is now freed of the endless book work and administration for which he was not ordained. Now he can devote himself to the preaching of the Gospel either literally or symbolically by his community actions. The times have called for this shift away from the one man rule to the collegiality of the circle of believers.

A heavy dose of clerical domination over the centuries had been fed to the layman. This is why there is still doubt about the layman being connected with the Church whether in or out of the sanctuary. This, however, is really only a prejudice. Laymen have a long tradition of being associated with the Church and today's situation calls for his return. The pyramid-to-the-circle is today's formula for a successful parish. Indeed, as the late Archbishop of Atlanta, Paul Hallihan has said, the recent definition of the Church itself as an open circle is "a correction—a rediscovery of the Gospels—what God wants His Church to be. In other times, other shapes may have been effective, but in a world grown used to self reliance, dialogue, involvement, and the democratic way of life, the pyramid will not do. The 'open circle' is scripturally authentic and historically appropriate."

Let us extend our remarks in one further comment. When the Archbishop said that the circle concept is scripturally authentic he was referring to Christ's own approach to His beginning Church—and it is good that those still uneasy about the "emerging layman" should take note of this. From the start Jesus took to himself his twelve apostles. They were united to Him first by believing in Him, then hoping in Him and then loving Him. Next they were most closely united with Him through baptism in an almost physical way. At the Last Supper this union became complete. They became a united body which we call the Mystical Body, a circle of intimate people living with the same life that is Christ's. St. Paul, as you know, likened our mystic union with Christ to that of a human body. He said, "As the body is but one while having many parts, and as all the parts of the body, however many they are, form but a single unity, so it is with Christ." (1 Cor 12:22) In this he was echoing Jesus himself who talked in terms of the Vine and the Branches saying that there were many parts but only one tree. These figures of speech such as the body and the vine support the original close community concept of priest and people. They indicate a collegiality of unity, love and fraternity.

Historical circumstances frequently forced the pastor to Leader on Top of the Pyramid, but his real role has always been as spiritual Father and Presider over the community love and community worship. Thus the changing parish structure of today reflects this. The pastor is resuming more fully his former role as community focalizer and the people are resuming their role as co-sharers in the apostolate and co-workers of the Christian community. Vatican II has strongly supported this concept both in word and in work. In the decree of the Laity we find words such as these:

> Lay people have also been made sharers in the priestly, prophetic and royal office of Christ (art. 2). . . . Within the communities of the Church, their cooperation is so

much needed that without it the apostolate of the pastors would be largely ineffectual. . . . We desire that lay people in the parish work in close cooperation with their priests, that they bring to this assembly of the Church their own problems and the questions of the world relating to salvation, for common study and resolution (art. 10). . . . In dioceses, as far as possible, there should be councils which assist the apostolic work of the Church either in the field of making the Gospel known and men holy, or in the charitable, social or other spheres. To this end, clergy and religious should appropriately cooperate with the laity. While preserving the proper character and autonomy of each organization, these councils will be able to promote the mutual coordination of various lay associations and enterprises. . . .

To this end we are aware of how Pope Paul brought into existence the Synod of Bishops to help him in the ruling of the Universal Church. We are aware that many dioceses have councils of laymen and priests for this same purpose. Parishes are merely reflecting this pattern when both pastor and laymen restructure the pyramid and sit down in a circle to discuss the People of God.

— 2 —

A final word ought to be said about future changes and extensions of the parish structure. As we saw in the first part of this chapter, the layers of the old time parish "pyramid" have reshifted and even, in some cases, disappeared. The parish was once that "mighty fortress" to which the faithful came. It was, without any irreverence intended, a kind of spiritual filling station, available in quiet or splendid isolation to those who would and could come. It had little time and little relation to the rest of the community. It was, rather, a city within a city. Social concerns of the community were not its interests. The label was conspicuously "Catholic" and those of other faiths or no faiths had to fend for themselves in any domestic or social problems.

This old-time defensive and isolationist type parish is giving way as we have seen, and the emphasis is on social commitment. More and more parishes are not asking "What is good for St. Joe's or St. Monica's," but rather "What is good for this town, this community of which we are a part?" With the new shift (as we shall see in another chapter) to social morality and social consciousness, parishes will become more and more orientated to the town in which they exist. Parishes more and more will be reaching out to community concerns, cooperating with other religious and secular bodies in fighting racism, poverty, hunger and ignorance. More Catholics will sit on boards of education, and this will include priests and sisters. More Catholics will take part in secular social programs. Again, this is reflecting the movement away from the pyramid to the circle, a renewed awareness that the parish itself is a community of worshipers who cannot be indifferent to the needs of their brothers.

Along this line, the Catholic will witness more experimental types of parishes, parishes geared to the needs of particular groups. Territorial lines will not be important for those parishes that may come into being for conservative or for liberal groups; or for those of a particular profession or those who wish more liturgical experimentation. Even now, parishes are being set up in the inner city and may be no more than a store front church. It's this type of parish that represents a moving out to the people rather than having them come to the parish, something that non-Catholics or the hostile are not likely to do. In this inner city type parish priests may rent an apartment for their "rectory"; they may be interested, not in direct conversions, but in simply helping people and particularly the underprivileged by just being a sign of Christian concern to them.

There are already some "shared-ministry" parishes where the two or three priests are equals, each taking as his territory a particular part of the parish. Each may live in his own home or apartment and meet together for consulation. Freed of a regular parish church and school and therefore very often freed of a large debt and the worriment over money such priests are more able to move around and give personal service to the people.

Because of the shortage of priests, deacons may be a permanent part of the future parish structure. There are already training centers and some dioceses already have some men under training. So serious is this step that there exists a booklet put out by the Bishops' Conference information director giving not only the background, history and the steps being taken to restore the permanent diaconate, but it also includes the names and addresses of the present (1970) six United States training centers. ("Permanent Deacons: Who, What, Why," USCC Publications Office, 1312 Massachusetts Ave., NW, Washington, D.C. 20005.)

We can only hazard a guess as to what the parish of the future will be, but it is probably safe to say that it will remain pretty much the way it was externally, except that it will have a more shared control and assistance in the form of Parish Councils and deacons, it will

be more community orientated and, within its boundaries, it may contain smaller free-floating cultural or
specialized parishes geared to specific needs.

— 3 —

If the Parish Council is replacing a strictly one-man
rule in many parishes, this is not always evident and
visible to the people. What is more visible and more upsetting in parish life to many is the absence or decline
of parish devotions. People don't even bring their missals to Mass anymore, and that's as good a sign as any
that something's "wrong" with parish devotions. Perhaps, to get at the bottom of the evaporting devotions,
we ought to stop right there, at the missals. A word on
the disappearing missal will help us see the dynamics
involved in the Novenas, Rosaries, etc.

The people's missal, as a matter of history, is only
about fifty years old. This usually startles the average
Catholic who somehow pictures the saints throughout
the ages going to Mass with missals tucked under their
arms. But no, the priest was the only one who used the
missal. One reason was that often he was the only man
in town who could read the language in which the Mass
was written. In the middle ages the text of the Mass was
in the book called the Sacramentary. This was used ex-
clusively by the priest since, by that time, he had taken
over the people's parts anyway. Besides, the people
knew by heart some prayers like the "Lord have mercy"
and the "Gloria." There was another book used at Mass,
the Lectionary, and this contained the Epistle and Gospel readings and that was all.

Only after the Council of Trent (16th century) did
we finally get what we know as the missal. Even then,

the missal was in Latin and printers were forbidden to produce it in the language of the people. Missals in the people's language did not appear until 1897 in foreign countries. This may seem strange to us who were used to a great variety of missals, but Rome seemed to think that it had good reasons for not allowing vernacular missals until two centuries after Trent. Politics had a lot to do with it. A certain French translation was condemned in 1660. The threat of the Jansenist heresy and the threat to the unity of the Church by the Protestant Reformers were other factors.

In any case, by the middle of the last century these reasons had lost their validity and a widespread movement for a vernacular missal began in Europe. In the United States in the 1920's a representative of a publishing company in St. Paul, Minnesota went to the Archbishop to ask his advice on publishing a missal in English. He finally received permission and thus came into being the pioneer St. Andrew's Daily Missal in the 1920's. For the first time Americans had an English missal. Others soon followed like the St. Joseph's, the Maryknoll missal and Fr. Lasance's. The biggest impetus in our country to the English missal was given by a Brooklyn priest, Father Joseph Stedman who was the first to produce low-cost novena booklets and then missals. This was the well done little Mass pocketbook that went with our soldiers all over the world during World War II. After World War II the use of the missal was firmly entrenched.

It might be noted here that there were certain undesirable side effects however: since the priest's prayers were also in the missal the people got used to reading his part (perhaps getting back at him for stealing *their* parts) and, secondly, it made the people *readers* instead of doers and participators; Vatican II has tried to offset this with the New Mass which shares the parts of worship among the priest and people.

How many people really know this history? How many are aware that the old missal goes back only fifty years? Once more, this interesting history of our beloved missal demonstrates fluctuations in our Church habits and the changes in our devotions. It prepares us to assess other parish devotions in the past and present in the expectation of changes in the future. (It should also make us pause and see how quick we are to equate a forty or fifty year old tradition with "that's the way it *always* was.")

Anyway, that changes have occurred is beyond dispute. As symbolic as anything else it is worth recording that a little devotional weekly called *Novena Notes* ceased publication a few years ago for the very reason that the Novena had so declined that there was no call for it anymore. At the Catholic Press conventions the publishers of devotional books don't even display devotional books anymore. Many feel sad at this development and see in this a decline of personal piety.

Of course, the old pyramid church as a solemn and solitary citadel housing the Eucharistic Lord was once the drawing power for the average Catholic. As a passive refuge in a hostile culture it drew the people who came in silence to worship God at Mass, visits, forty hours, novenas and confession. The immigrant people were trained in habits of regularity and routine. The repetition of prayers such as litanies, novenas, the rosary and the angelus reflected this training. It was inevitable however, that throughout the ages, more mystery and ceremony should surround these things. Since the Mass itself was largely unintelligible it was natural that people turned to these devotions and surrounded them with pomp and pageantry which was as bewildering to the non-Catholic as comforting to the Catholic. But these devotions had a comforting, lulling effect and gave great security.

Then things changed suddenly. Vatican II promoted the upheaval (though by no means did it invent it). The Council's stress on the return to active lay participation in the Mass and its emphasis on Scripture necessarily undermined the nonliturgical devotions. But when one remembers that the nonliturgical devotions were a reaction to and a replacement for an unintelligible Mass liturgy, perhaps this was only poetic justice. The newly educated laity were not at home with many of the old country holdovers. The younger people, impatient of routine prayer and regularity, made fun of their parent's or grandparent's "superstition." They rushed in to fill the gap with Bible vigils and other "meaningful" replacements, some ridiculous, others quite sensible and relevant. It is in the crush of such postconciliar adjustments that the ordinary devotions of the parish have almost come to a halt. We are still awaiting the outcome, but at least we see the dynamics of history that have brought the situation about.

While we await the outcome, there are several thoughts that can guide and sustain us. First of all, in the long run the Church will hold on to those devotions that are truly meaningful. Any novelties that are around will be shortlived, others that help will endure. The rosary which has declined in popularity, will probably regain its popularity perhaps in another form. Secondly, those devotions which are disappearing may really no longer serve any use and they are better leaving the scene. Again, as in the case of our missals, this is a change that should cause no surprise. For example, several devotions of past ages no longer serve any purpose today. Pilgrimages for one thing. Public acts of penance which used to be so popular. We no longer have public processions that were around for years and years. Massive religious rallies have pretty much faded from the scene.

As time goes on and things settle our parish devotional life will return readjusted and re-formed. By this time the false polarization will have gone by the board, the polarization of those with the either-or mentality; either we have concelebrated Mass or novena; either we have an offertory procession or a May procession. This either-or mentality is unwarranted. There is no reason why in Holy Mother Church room cannot be made for both. There will always be room in the Church for devotions. However, we can expect from a TV raised, multi-media public new tastes and new approaches.

CHAPTER IV

The Good Old Days

– 1 –

Liturgical changes, parish changes, change all over the place. Many a Catholic, caught in the confusion of transition, has cast a longing eye on what becomes more and more appealing with each new change: "the good old days." These were the days when the Church was the Church, when people knew where they stood, when everything was crystal clear, there were black and white rules and the attitude was "take them or leave them." The Pope reigned in peace and the members of the Holy Roman Catholic Church obeyed with joyful submission. With such a tableau enshrined in the hearts of many it is no wonder there is a looking back, that there is evidence of a Catholic nostalgia for the stability and serenity of the past.

But is this tableau accurate? Was the past really like that? Does history back this up or is there some foundation to the suspicion that for some those "good old days" go back only forty or fifty years? To get an idea of the truth of the matter, let us take a quick glance at the past using the general councils of the Church to focus our attention. Since these councils were responses to the needs and crises of their times then, better than anything else, they can show us the realities of history.

The First General Council was held in 325 in Nicaea,

a present day village in Turkey. It was called in response to a certain Arius who said that Christ was not God. To us subdued Westerners this would be a serious but academic controversy. But to the Easterners of the early centuries any heresy was a cause for intrigue, accusation, counter accusation, politics, fighting and rioting among the ordinary people. If Christ were not God, what about His saving death on the cross and what was sinful man to hope for after death? The people had the intuition of what the great Protestant scholar Adolph Harnack later said when he observed that if Arianism had been victorious it would have ruined Christianity completely, emptying it of all religious content. Anyway, from the emperor to the meanest street cleaner, all must be interested both personally and, in the manner of the East, passionately. This first council was called to heal this greatest rift in the early Church; and, again, this was not merely an academic rift among theologians but involved bloody rioting and terrible fighting in city after city as the controversy raged. In fact, a second general council had to be called in Constantinople in 381 to reaffirm the belief as summarized in the Nicene creed and reaffirm the stand against Arianism.

Another council was necessary also because the religious questions were kept alive by powerful emperors who, from the earliest times, began a voluntary sort of protectorate over the Church and, in the course of history, several times nearly "protected" her out of existence. One of Constantine's sons, Constantius II, was an Arian and with great violence and persecution gave Arianism a new lease on life. A later emperor, Valens (365-78), also renewed the heresy and loosed a persecution upon the Catholics.

The Fourth General Council of the Church, held at Chalcedon in 451, besides responding to the heresies which denied that Christ has two natures, had some interesting side decrees which reveal a not totally happy state of affairs. For example, clergy are forbidden to join the army, they must not marry heretics and they will be penalized if they take part in any abductions.

Again, to show how seriously the Easterners took their religion, as a prelude to the Fifth General Council held in 553 at Constantinople, a whole army had to be brought in to get the lawful bishop of Jerusalem back to his see. Troops had to be used to get still another bishop back to his see of Alexandria. Even then the mobs turned on the troops and when they took refuge in a church the mob burned it down. Later, still incensed, the mob finally murdered the unfortunate bishop and his naked, mutilated corpse was dragged through the streets in triumph.

Nor was this the only high-pitched experience in the daily life of the Church. Preceding the calling of the sixth council against the Monothelites, an emperor (Constans II) in the year 653 had the pope himself kidnapped, carried bodily from before the high altar of St. Peter's, loaded with chains and shipped as a common criminal to Constantinople. He was thrown into a dungeon and later tried for "treason" for plotting to keep property from the emperor. The pope was jailed again and finally exiled where he died.

The Seventh General Council was no less stormy and the issues were no less highly penetrating in the lives of the ordinary Christian. (Again, our Western minds and our Anglo-Saxon aloofness make it difficult to see how such issues would involve the man in the street, but they did. These theological controversies were the civil rights and anti-war movements of their day.) This council dealt with the venerating of images, an issue brought about by the Emperor Leo nicknamed with obviousness, the "iconoclast," the "imagebreaker." He felt strongly that image use and veneration were watering down Christianity and an outright danger. Thus he set about to wipe out this practice with a vengeance. Those who opposed him suffered cruelly if they did not forswear (as did the patriarch of Constantinople) the veneration of images or the invoking of the saints. It was only as the result of this council that the whole problem was settled but not without bloodshed. The words of the pope summarized the final doctrine, "With regard to images, the belief of St. Gregory and our belief are the same; and so the Greek bishops themselves, in this very synod, accepted the definition, to reverence images with salutations of honor, but by no means to give to them that true worship which, according to our faith, we give to the divine nature alone. . . ."

The Eighth General Council in 868 dealt with the origins of one of the great rifts in the Catholic Church: the antipathy of the East and West and the ultimate breaking away of the Greek from the Latin Church. The far reaching consequences of what started to focalize in the ninth century came to a head in the eleventh and finally reached its culmination in that shattering tragedy, the fall of Constantinople in 1453. The present issue, though severe, was then just the beginning: who was the lawful patriarch of Constantinople, Photius or Ignatius? The ensuing intrigues, misunderstandings, excommunications and counter-excommunications only served to lay the groundwork for the inevitable tragedies just mentioned.

The Ninth General Council of 1123 was the first one

to be held in the West, at Rome itself. It, too, was the end result of severe abuses culminating in and symbolized by an era of bad popes. There were three major problems of the time. First was simony whereby a price tag was put on everything ecclesiastical whatever, from the hearing of confessions to payments for being ordained a priest. Next there was clerical immorality. Clerical marriage, quite common and illicit, was very much tied to property and wealth and the sons of priests and bishops so took over their benefices and church property as to make them family endowments. The third and final evil of the time which was to plague the Church for a long time was the problem of lay investiture whereby the emperor or local kings virtually and often directly appointed bishops to their sees. A long line of reformers were to use at times almost obscene language to describe these three evils—evils which weren't really cleared up with any finality until the Council of Trent in the sixteenth century.

And once more in all of these matters the daily life of the average Christian was quite affected. In trying to come to terms with such problems as lay control of church appointments, simony, etc., matters spilled over into the streets. In 1075 in Milan, for example, half the city with its cathedral was burned down over these issues. Still the emperor continued to appoint his men as bishops, the pope deposed the emperor (unheard of up to that time), *his* bishops in turn deposed the pope; finally the emperor put his man on the papal throne and the real pope (Gregory VII) had to flee from Rome and later died in exile; and after his death for three years Christendom was without a pope at all. The Concordat of Worms in 1122 officially ended the lay investiture quarrel but by no means ended the problem. The Ninth

General Council incorporated the victories of the Concordat in its canons.

Although the Tenth General Council in 1139 had to deal with the immediate crisis that there were two popes around, it is interesting to look at some of the decrees promulgated as a fair assessment of the troubles of the times. For example, it is henceforth decreed that clerics who marry (which shows the persistency of the problem of which there are echoes today) were not validly married; clerics must not leave to their sons church property; the ancient custom that the public was permitted to go in and plunder a deceased bishop's house was to cease; those who set fires and burn down places are not to be forgiven without heavy penances and (interestingly) new-fangled weapons such as the catapult that hurls huge masses of stone are condemned as being "detested by God." (It is tempting to think what this Council would have to say about the nuclear bomb and napalm.)

The Twelfth General Council is considered one of the greatest in the Church; it is the Fourth Council of the Lateran in 1215. Its main achievements are a series of reforming laws and doctrinal pronouncements which again indicate serious flaws in daily Christian life and the presence of heresies—in this case Manicheism and Albigensianism, forms of excessive Puritanism. Its disciplinary laws are again revealing: there are heavy penalties against drunken clergy and those who never say Mass. Clerics should not enter the army or act as surgeons, go on stage, shoot dice or frequent taverns. Bishops must not receive money from those whom they are absolving from excommunication and the sacraments are to be given without charge. The use of relics which had gotten out of hand, is regulated and all must confess their sins once a year and make their Easter duty. Priests are not to reveal what they hear in confession under pain of being thrust into a severe monastery, there to do penance for the rest of their lives.

— 2 —

The thirteenth and fourteenth centuries which saw the councils of Lyons (1245 and 1274) and Vienne (1311) also saw the ever recurring contest between popes and emperors (witness Innocent IV fleeing Italy in disguise) and the invention of the now familiar conclave, the rule by which papal electors are locked up until they have chosen a pope. It was the Council of Constance in 1414, however, that had to deal with another great tragedy in the Church: the Great Schism whereby there were two and then three simultaneously reigning popes! In solving this problem it raised another, never altogether solved and indeed alive in the collegial considerations of today, that is, the relationship of the pope to the council and ultimately his place among the other bishops.

It was during this century that in 1377 Gregory XI returned to Rome. He and other popes had been "prisoners" at Avignon in France for seventy years. It was the terrible scolding of St. Catherine of Siena that forced Gregory back into the Eternal City. This general period also typifies many of the normal tensions of the times so that Henri Daniel-Rops, the Catholic historian can describe the fourteenth century as a time of crisis: "the crisis of authority, the crisis of unity and, conditioning both, the crisis in men's souls, in their consciences and in their minds." The authority crisis was centered, as we saw, around the scandal of having three men claiming the papacy at the same time. The crisis of unity centered around the physical dismemberment of the Church with the invasion of the Turks and the Fall of Constantinople in 1453. The crisis in men's souls was reflected in the lack of balance in religion. This was the era of horrific art; the era of an outrageous preoccupation with the Passion of Christ and its physical terrors; the time of unsettled mysticism which passed over into superstition. Daniel-Rops describes it thus:

> This unbalanced mysticism and exacerbated symbolism mingled with a realism which was also part of the spirit of the times: the sublime brushed shoulders with the ridiculous. When eating an apple one pious individual would divide the fruit into four pieces, munching the first three in honor of the Trinity and the last in memory of the food which Mary had offered the Child Jesus. . . . Another devout soul would drink a glass of wine in five gulps, in memory of the five wounds of Christ. . . . In Germany there were statuettes of the crucified Christ containing a bladder filled with blood, which was made to flow realistically through the five wounds; and several figures of the Virgin possessed a shutter in the stomach which, when opened, revealed the Holy Child in His mother's womb. . . .

This was the era when in spite of the rules of the Fourth Lateran Council veneration of the saints and relics reached the point of genuine superstition. In fact, there was no city of any size that did not boast of the possession of some relic. The city of Cologne, for instance, had in its cathedral the remains of the Three Magi! Charlemagne's burial place was said to contain the outer garments of the Blessed Virgin and the bloody cloth on which the head of St. John the Baptist rested. In France there were the "relics" of the crown of thorns, the lance that pierced Christ's side, the tablecloth used at the Last Supper and pieces of the tablet on which the Ten Commandments had been inscribed. The Castle Church in Wittenberg contained over five thousand relics including a piece of the Burning Bush in which God appeared to Moses and 204 parts of the bodies of the Holy Innocents. An indulgence of more than 1,443 years could be obtained by venerating these relics. Astrology also flourished at this period. The decadence of the clergy increased as well. Money lust, concubinage, absenteeism and clerical ignorance (many could not read or write) were still common complaints of the time. One has only to read the poet Dante to get a picture of medieval problems and disgraces which trickled down to the man in the street.

The Great Western Schism, as we have already taken note, shook the confidence of the people in the papacy and continuing corruptions in the Church caused good men to groan. Dolan, in his book *History of the Reformation* quotes at length a theologian of the day (14th century):

> What benefit or what usefulness does the magnificent glory of princes and the superfluous pomp of prelates and cardinals, unmindful that they are but men, confer upon the Church? Is it not detestable that one person should hold two hundred, another three hundred, ecclesiastical benefits? . . . Judge if it is even right that the books of the churches, and the like, are sometimes sold, and castles and houses mortgaged to pay to the collectors the exactions imposed by the bishops on the clergy. . . . Why is the means of earning a living from their own property not mercifully given to converted Jews? Instead they are compelled to live in extreme poverty, driven to apostatize and to accuse Christians of ungodliness. . . . What is the meaning of the fact . . . that even the bishops, lay aside their copes, surplices

and books, take up arms and, fully equipped, fight in
the fields like secular princes? . . . Why is it that today,
bishops, abbots and monks, rather than being ministers
of Christ, are fiscal officers. . . . Open your eyes and see
if any nunneries have today become prostitutes' houses,
if any monasteries, consecrated to God, have become
market places and taverns. . . . Make a careful examination and see if anywhere the priests have committed
illicit intercourse, having concubines under the pretext
of maidservants. Judge whether such a variety of
images and pictures in the churches is suitable and
whether it does not turn many people to a kind of idolatry. . . . And what practice could be more damnable
than this: the clerics and the laity, prelates and princes,
everywhere are so mad as to celebrate the most holy
night of the Nativity of Christ in playing dice. . . .

Things weren't like this all over, but it was a bad state
of affairs and did have an enormous influence in bringing about the Protestant Reformation.

There was the period—say, from the twelfth to the
fifteenth centuries—that the Church became over-
institutionalized and the Roman papacy became entrenched. Pope Boniface had gone so far as to claim that
he was the vicar not only of Peter and of Christ, but of
God Himself. He was the one who proclaimed that "for
every creature it was absolutely necessary for salvation
to be subject to the Roman Pontiff."

After this era there are the final three councils we
must mention. The Eighteenth General Council was
held under Julius II, Michelangelo's mentor and tor-
mentor, in 1512. This era was again a time of conflict between church and state, the state being this time Louis
XII of France and again, it was over land. Julius wanted
his own states in Italy and so conflict was inevitable.
The Council itself, however (continued under Leo X,

a Medici), was once more that of reform. There's a certain irony to this since only eight months after the Council's opening Martin Luther was to take reform out of theory and put it into practice. Among the reforms and canons brought forth were that of having a censor for books—a necessity, it was thought, since printing had recently been invented. Rules on preaching which had fallen into general disrepute were formed. Looting of cardinals' residences during the vacancies of the Holy See was forbidden!

The great Council of Trent was a reactive one: a reaction against the suddenness and depth of the Protestant Reformation. It was, at long last, *the* reforming council and it was reform or die. It was also the most theological, putting into precise form and wording Catholic belief, especially those under attack by the Protestants. It finally gave the death blow to the benefice system, bore down hard on the absentee priest, bishop or abbot, the gifts of money to bishops on visitations; firmly regulated indulgences (a sore point indeed!) especially in connection with money and the practice of nepotism; dealt with the training of the clergy and the regulation of marriage. Noteworthy also was a striking note of humility, hitherto absent but to reappear so forcefully in Vatican II. The great Cardinal Pole's keynote address ran with self-deprecating phrases:

> Let us come to what are called abuses. . . . It will be found that it is our ambition, our avarice, our cupidity that have wrought all these evils on the people of God. . . . Before the tribunal of God's mercy we, the shepherds, should make ourselves responsible for all the evils now burdening the flock of Christ . . . not in generosity, but in justice . . .

There was the era of the Inquisition and general intolerance (for both Catholics and Protestants). Dating
from the end of the sixteenth century all of Christendom
fell victim to the fire and the sword. Many countries
were engulfed in civil war over religious matters. In the
name of religion, men were beaten, burned at the stake,
hanged, quartered or beheaded—and all without a
qualm of conscience. And, as Daniel-Rops in his book
The Catholic Reformation says sadly, "Painful as it may
be to a follower of the God of Love, one thing is beyond
question: responsibility for this manifold tragedy must
be attributed to religion" (p.149).

The seventeenth century saw the religious Thirty
Years War and the rise of Jansenism and Quietism. The
eighteenth century saw the condemnation of Galileo,
the rise of the rationalists led by Voltaire and the suppression of the Jesuits. On Christmas Eve, 1775 Pius VI
published his encyclical *Inscrutabile divinae sapientiae
consilium* listing the problems of the Church at the time
and lamenting that faith had been shaken, irreligion was
making rapid strides and morality had become unstable.
The beginning of the nineteenth century already saw
the Church in the throes of the French Revolution.

Finally, it was the First Vatican Council that tried to
come to terms with the newly arising sciences, tried to
find a synthesis between faith and reason and finally
came up with the carefully worded and much disputed
(ecclesiastically and politically) teaching on papal infallibility which today, in the light of Vatican II, is undergoing interpretation and adjustment as the realities
of collegiality define themselves.

In our own United States two movements in our
young country early brought severe crisis. The first was
lay trusteeism which appeared about 1785 and which,

as late as the Civil War, found laymen in some Eastern and Southern dioceses offering grave challenges to Church authority. This was the situation when laymen held the parish purse strings and tried to hire and fire their pastors. The second American crisis was known as Americanism and was present in the closing days of the last century. This was the suspicion by the Catholic Europeans that doctrine in America was not quite orthodox. The European simply did not understand the American way of life and religious pluralism and in fact Leo XIII issued a letter *Testem benevolentiae* which condemned ideas that passed as Americanism among certain Europeans. This whole question caused quite some dissension among the American bishops and clergy.

— 3 —

The point of this hop-skip-and-jump through the pages of history is to make the reader re-think the concept of the "good old days." Suppose, for example, you were a Catholic in the fourth century when a great deal of genuine acrimony involved the average citizen in the Arian heresy. And you would be involved somehow on one side or another. The mentality of the people of the first centuries was such that they took religion seriously and heresy was a realistic and everyday affair. No one was indifferent. That's why St. Jerome in 359 complained, "The whole world groaned and marveled at finding itself Arian." Suppose you lived in the unenlightened times of the fifth century when terrible repressive measures were taken against heretics who could not build churches, hold meetings, teach their doctrine even in private; who were disqualified from making wills, inheriting estates, entering into financial contracts, banished, scourged and put to death.

Suppose you lived in the eighth century when everyone was quarrelling over the use of images and statues or in the ninth century when celibacy was such a dead issue that bishops and priests not only openly married but bequeathed church property to their children. Or in the tenth century which saw no less than twenty-five popes; or in the thirteenth century when the Christian Crusades sacked Constantinople thus earning the eternal grudge of the Greeks ever since. Suppose you lived at any point in the Middle Ages and discovered that your priest could neither read nor write; or you had to pay taxes to a prince-bishop who was never in his diocese; or you witnessed four- or five-year-old cardinals running around; or saw Alexander VI or one of those several bad popes riding off to the hunt with one of his mistresses? Suppose you were a Catholic in the hectic days of the Crusades or that you witnessed the spectacle of first two and then three popes reigning simultaneously. Suppose you were a part of the years of the Protestant Reformation when whole nations were overturned religiously, when intolerance was the order of the day, when you had to choose the religion of your local king. Or you were caught in the blood bath of the French Revolution. Or even if you lived in the last century you would have witnessed Pius IX being accused of being a Freemason, his Secretary of State being assassinated and the pope fleeing Rome and on his return making himself a voluntary prisoner of the Vatican. At this time also, as a Catholic in Germany you would be feeling the pinch of persecution known as the *Kulturkampf*. Even before these modern days of multimedia communications, you would somehow have been affected and maybe seriously so.

On the other hand there is the possibility that you may have been fortunate enough to live in between the larger moments of religious historical upsetment and only feel the stress of the times indirectly. Or, most fortunately, you may have been sheltered from much and have lived in one of those quiet pockets of tranquility and holiness which have also always been a part of the Church's history just as there have always been wonderful saints and holy and sincere Catholics.

Actually, the "good old days" nostalgia has a tenuous basis in the fact that most Catholics over thirty in this country have been raised in a relatively stable and religiously peaceful time. Such Catholics might recall the social problems such as the Depression of '29 and World Wars I and II. Religiously, however, the period of the last fifty or sixty years for the average middle class Catholic was stable enough. As we saw in the previous chapter he had his church with its regular round of devotions, his priests and his parochial school. Authority was rigid and paternal reflecting the prevailing pattern of the day. There was the strict and secure party line in matters religious. Rules were clear cut: one didn't eat meat on Fridays, one went to church on Sundays and one did not practice birth control or marry Protestants ever. If the Church had always known crisis it was not evident to the Catholic of the immediate past. Because it wasn't he tended to romanticize what went before and to refer to this vague era as the "good old days." In this our own day, as we are passing through the customary crisis that historically is an aftermath of every Church General Council, the "good old days" have taken on particular appeal. But, as we have seen, that phrase is not accurate and history belies it. We may indeed yearn for the periods we knew in our growing up, those periods of peace and standardization, but we should not romanticize the past, even the immediate past, into something it was not. Monsignor Hughes is right: our Church is a Church in Crisis. Vatican II is historically right: our Church is that "Pilgrim Church" struggling through history and, like all pilgrims, getting considerable dust on her shoes in the process.

— 4 —

To add more emphasis to the fallacy of the "good old days" we must include some interesting tidbits about our strictly religious practices and devotional life. In a kind of "Did-You-Know?" routine, let us run down the list: Did you know, for example:

— that for the first several centuries, there were many different liturgies, many different ways of offering Mass and dispensing the sacraments?

— that right up to the sixth century Holy Communion was still being given out under both species although the rule of St. Columban decreed that uncouth persons and novices in religious orders should receive Communion under the form of bread alone—which shows that they had problems way back then?

— that it was in the sixth century that the list of saints in the old Roman canon achieved its present form?

— that in the seventh century it was the practice in the Eastern rites to receive Communion in one's hand and communicate oneself?

— that priests of the eighth century celebrated Mass as often as they wished? Pope Leo III himself offered as many as seven Masses on a single feast day.

— that during this period Holy Communion was received only two or three times a year?

— that in the eighth century was introduced the small, white round shaped host we know today? That before that ordinary loaves of unleavened bread were used in the Mass?

— that in the tenth century the Roman liturgy finally prevailed in the Western world but up until that time many differences were still prevalent in the way Mass was offered and the sacraments given?

— that in the eleventh century it was finally settled by Pope Nicholas II that only the cardinal bishops should have a hand in running the papal elections?

— that it was only in the eleventh century that the Nicene Creed was universally added to the Roman Mass?

— that in the eleventh century the use of incense (formerly rejected as pagan) was introduced into Mass and that the Commemoration of the dead on All Souls day made its appearance?

— that in the twelfth century, under Pope Innocent III the subdiaconate became a major order towards the priesthood?

— that the Breviary that the priest reads every day became official in the Roman Church only in the thirteenth century?

— that the fourteenth century saw the introduction of Exposition of the Most Blessed Sacrament and also the Stations of the Cross?

— that the angelus was introduced as a custom in the fifteenth century?

— that the rosary itself was also a product of the fifteenth century being proclaimed by the Dominican Alan de Rupe?

— that the Hail Mary did not receive its final form until the sixteenth century?

— that the First Fridays were not a part of Catholic life until the nineteenth century?

— that First Communion for children of seven did not come until the twentieth century?

Things like this catch the average Catholic up short. That such things should startle them has been the fault of those who have taught them. They have unwillingly perpetrated a myth of a "Fortress Church" floating somehow several feet above the ground untouched by human history and uninhabited by human beings; a fortress already firmly fixed with no potential to grow and develop. Such an image is not the Church of Christ who reminded us that no servant is above his Master—and we have always known what men have done to Him.

Actually, the real and genuine nostalgia should be the realization that, as one pages through history, the Holy Spirit has so obviously been present bringing brightness out of darkness and renewal out of what appears to be the death of the Church. St. Bernard of Clairvaux once said, "Who will give me to see before I die the Church of God as in the good old days when the apostles spread their nets to take not gold or silver but the souls of men." He was reflecting on the terrible conditions of his day and looked to the past. But, in spite of his times, he was a saint thus proving that men cannot stifle the Spirit of God altogether. It is possible that, as in the past, our present changes are the symptoms of genuine development in the Church. Thus for us who are going through one of those frequent historical difficulties, when we are experiencing the throes of change as the space age continues to open wider we should look back only to the promise of Christ Who said that He would be with us all days, "even to the end of the world." So far He has kept that promise.

CHAPTER V

Was I Taught Wrong?

— 1 —

At this point, we must introduce a critical chapter in our investigation of change. This will be crucial because it deals basically with a serious underlying concern of the Middle Catholic caught up in a renewal he doesn't really understand: that of frustration. We refer to that frustration which results not only from discovering how much the liturgy has changed over the centuries or from encountering the emerging layman or even from taking a second look at those good old days; but we refer to that frustration which encounters matters of doctrine and teaching. They—meaning everyone and anyone, official and unofficial who keep coming up with something new—they say there is no such thing as Original Sin, that there weren't any Magi following any star at all, that you don't have to go to confession anymore or not as often, that there is no such thing as mortal sin anyway, that priests can marry, that the pope isn't in charge any more, that birth control is all right if you think so, that premarital sex is permitted, that eating meat on Fridays is allowed and women don't have to wear hats to church.

This accumulated list of real or imagined changes, this combination of the serious and the trivial is symptomatic of the deep frustration that many people, especially the older generation, feel; and this feeling takes the form of considering oneself cheated. There is that sinking sensation resulting from the sudden realization that one was obviously taught all wrong in the past. "Did my Church lie to me?" asks the Middle Catholic, "If it wasn't right then, is it right now? Can I really ever trust the Church again? All of a sudden I'm wrong! All of a sudden all the things that I was taught as true without deviation or hesitation, without qualification or explanation—they are not true any more! There's no other word for it: I feel cheated!"

This sense of frustration is probably more widespread than is realized. Those who get this feeling either blindly and quietly cling to the old or become militant against the new. Sometimes, to be truthful, this sense of frustration is not easily dispelled simply because there are no answers to some good questions. Sometimes everything *does* seem relative and no matter what they say about the development of doctrine and seeing the Church in its present day context, there seems to be no more room for old, transcendental truths and unassailable dogmas. And thus arises that old feeling of bewilderment and even anger that what was wrong then is all right now and vice versa. And when it comes to something as personal and demanding as, say, birth control, then the frustration reaches its high point.

Let's try to get some understanding about all of this. We will offer considerations under two major headings: "We" and "You." By "We" we mean anyone who has taught in the name of the Church; we mean official and unofficial Church teaching and teachers from the Sunday morning sermon to the teacher in the parochial school; from a well defined dogma to an undefined "atmosphere" of what things were necessary to identify one as a Catholic and to get to heaven. By "You" we mean all the general people, the average Catholic, the man-in-the-street Catholic, those on the receiving end of the teaching.

First, we are to blame for present day frustrations because we taught religion without qualification. We did not do this out of malice, of course, but out of a misdirected concern for our spiritual children who, we forgot, had grown up. We found it easier simply to teach such and such a thing without qualification because qualifications would only confuse the issues and the people weren't ready for such sophistication; they were not up to all these distinctions. As we said, this was done without malice and was the result of a mentality that was a part of our heritage and social structure. We saw in the third chapter our own history in this country. We acknowledged our past immigrant standing, our little education, our language barrier, our immediate concern with earning a living, getting shorter working hours and fighting off the Protestants. There was little time for most people for leisure, for schooling, for fine distinctions. Doctrine, like life itself, was direct. A rural feudal mentality, imported from Europe, was still in effect; paternalism was still the order of society.

When it came to religion, we (the teachers) proved children of our time. We taught a preoccupied immigrant people in simple terms and in direct quotations. It was felt that the people were not ready for a lot of refinements and theories and distinctions. Such things were, of course, always there, kind of like being in the footnotes, but it was considered dangerous and unnecessary to dwell on them. Besides a strict party line was needed against those others (Protestants). All right, never mind that for centuries there were other interest-

ing theories on Original Sin or that some of the early
Fathers spoke of several first parents. Never mind that
St. Augustine taught a Darwinian form of evolution;
never mind that the moral manuals had an unusual
amount of excuses for legitimately missing Mass on
Sundays. Never mind that a hundred years ago the Ger-
mans and French in their monasteries were doing
strange things with the liturgy. Never mind that the
confessional box actually went back to Trent or that
there is no record of children's confessions ever being
heard before the fourteenth century. Never mind that
they used to give the left over sacred species of bread
and wine to infants. Never mind that people used to
communicate themselves. Never mind the late origin of
many of our religious customs which we saw at the end
of the last chapter. Never mind creative attempts to present the new. Never mind any of these things. Yes, they
were true but, really, it was safer to give one way, one
theory, one custom as absolute truth and practice and
not confuse the people. In fact, books that would confuse them or endanger them were often put on the
Index.

In her enlightening book *Prophets and Guardians*
Meriol Trevor makes a pertinent comment on Pius X's
efforts and the efforts of the Holy Office to squelch the
Modernists' errors by trying to control the scholars and
censor their writings:

> The usual defense of Pius X and his advisers is that
> they were acting on behalf of the "little ones" whose
> faith was threatened by the Modernists. Christ's warn-
> ing, addressed to those who mistreat children, was
> taken by ecclesiastical rulers to include adult but sim-
> ple members of the Church. But were Loisy's exegetical
> studies a terrible danger to the fishermen of Brittany?

Would Blondel's philosophy, almost incomprehensible to his friends, upset the peasants of Provence? If the little ones were the bourgeois capable of reading books of criticism, was a condemnation the best way of answering the questions raised? If it was necessary to crush Modernism in order to preserve the faith, what sort of faith, what sort of faithful were envisaged? When Cardinal Richard censured *L'Evangile et L'Eglise*, Loisy's sales doubled. After Tyrrell was dismissed from the Society of Jesus, his books commanded a wider public than before. People wanted to know what the fuss was about—they always do. Suppression of criticism and of new ideas, never easy since the invention of printing, was quite impossible by the beginning of the twentieth century. No one in authority would admit the questions, let alone provide what could have subdued Loisy's influence—better answers than his. Persistent refusals to face these questions surely meant that it would become harder for educated Catholics to remain believing Christians. And if Rome was willing to jettison the educated in order to preserve the faith of the simple, it was short-sighted not to realize that as more and more received education, so the problems would be revived on a wider scale and would not be less difficult to solve for the passage of time (p. 80).

Well, the passage of time took place and no one (in the Church-teaching circles) ever even noticed. Thus, we continued to teach without the proper qualifications, we held back, by giving only one view on a doctrine or custom where actually there were many; we proposed only one school of thought on revelation; we tapped only one source of tradition; we continued to lump together Church home-made laws with the laws of God and the deposit of faith. And we continued to censor out both the scholars and their new ideas. The result of all of this was to harden into a kind of absolute dogma what was in fact theory.

We of the teaching side always knew there were other schools of thought. Better educated laymen were exposed to them. But the average Catholic on the street, he was given one, uninhibited and simple truth for his uninhibited and simple mind. When Miss Trevor's assessment eventually came true and more and more people became educated; when they began to perceive other notable theories and traditions of our religion; when the old, hidden diversions of thought and practice surfaced at Vatican II, then the average, unprepared Catholic was upset and scandalized. He felt that "unassailable" doctrine was being assailed when it was often only a case of another traditional aspect of the same truth being revived. Thus, is our contention true: we are to blame for the uneasiness today because we so often taught religion without qualification.

Secondly, we have a history of being fearful. This fear stems from what we said above. If the people learned too much they might lose their faith. With such fear inevitably comes restriction, censorship and the closed mind. Thus the Church, once the patron of the arts and sciences, became suspicious of them. We learned nothing from the Galileo case, invented the Index of forbidden books, scoffed at Darwin, made fun of Freud and condemned Margaret Sanger. We were not alone of course. All organized religion in the Western world had reached varying degrees of bureaucratic closemindedness and fear; and fear as usual, brooked no deviation and thus ghettoism and isolationism and prejudice could flourish. As a result we made sharper divisions than really existed in our relationships with non-Catholics. We became accustomed to a black and white world. We became triumphant that we and we alone possessed the truth. We forged our own brand of discrimination. Again, not that anyone did this consciously. It was all the product of a mentality of the times, an aura we eased into by the simple process of being born into the kind of world that existed at the time. Whole nations of Catholics (at least nominally) could be indifferent, self-possessed and falsely righteous. In reading William Shirer's giant work *The Collapse of the Third Republic* one is struck, for example, at the rampant antisemitism of the Catholics in the horrid Dreyfus affair. Shirer quotes the daily Catholic weekly at the time, *La Croix* saying "Dreyfus is an agent of international Jewry which has decided to ruin the French people." Larger spirits in every country had to struggle against the official Church in their search for the truth and in the expression of the arts, and the Church had a long list of names under suspicion ranging from St. Thomas Aquinas to John Courtney Murray.

In short, being afraid that knowledge, little or much, was a dangerous thing for her subjects the Church taught a strict party line, forged the monolithic image, kept Protestantism at bay and thus protected herself from outside "corrupting" influences. But, of course, this proved to be not the best approach and as we moved from the age of fear to the age of education and from isolationism to ecumenism and from Vatican I to Vatican II the paucity of this tactic was obvious. Thus, again, we were to blame for not giving the newly educated Catholic credit to have enough identity to survive in a pluralistic society. We did not have enough confidence in the declaration of Pius X that the only fear the Church has is ignorance.

Thus, from the "We" side of the question, we have caused much of the present confusion and frustration by simply neglecting to realize that our Catholic children have grown up. It's an affliction of many mothers who are overly concerned and overly protective of their children. We were still treating our Catholic people as if the electronic age had not dawned and universal education had not arrived. We have consistently underestimated them. And now that widespread reading and in-depth education has revealed the wide variety of viewpoints and developments in the field of religion the oldsters are shocked, the youngsters belligerent and everyone is polarized unnecessarily. We, the teachers, are scrambling to re-tap the old, and re-present the new. The Middle Catholic is being caught in the ensuing confusion. We're branching out into new techniques and we're teaching the people many other aspects of our truly rich religious tradition. To those brought up in the one narrow tradition this is quite unsettling and brings up our "being cheated" slogan. The charge is more correct than first thought. But we are trying to make amends.

— 2 —

But we said there is another side, the "You" side and one must make some comments here. The one general comment to be made is that "you" (anyone on the receiving end of the teaching process) are not blameless. Granted that you were not encouraged to think for yourself; in fact, you were discouraged. Still, in this day and age, and for the past ten years, this has not been so. In fact, like every other department, religion too has had its knowledge explosion particularly after World War II. The question is: have you been doing your homework? have you read? have you taken courses in renewal? have you listened and opened your eyes and mind to what's going on?

Many people give their religious education such treatment that, if it were any other subject, they would not survive long in this world. To a great degree women keep up on fashions; men can recount major league standings with remarkable accuracy. Both know at least the names of the current best sellers, follow the TV with devotion, can pinpoint Saigon and give the names and ages of the Beatles. But religious education is another matter.

For many, formal religious education either stopped with Confirmation or their graduation from the Catholic high school. They live their lives, court their partners, marry their spouses, achieve success in their jobs, raise their families, advance their secular education—and, suddenly they find themselves at twenty-five or forty-five upset by all the happenings in the Church and all of the strange new doctrines. The newness is only new to those who learned the old some ten or forty years ago. Think seriously: when was the last time you took a religion course, read a religion explanation book through, sat through lectures on theology or kept up with the religiously informative magazines? (I won't even ask if you've read the documents of Vatican II!) You've kept up with a smattering of other things, but not religion. The appearance on the religious scene of some "new" theory or thought leaves you upset, makes you defensive and, cumulatively, gives you that sense of frustration, that feeling of being cheated that we spoke about above.

Being surprised at what's going on in the world of religion today—and from surprise taking the step to reaction—has its parallel in other fields. For example, there are a lot of things under wraps that various companies and different branches of science are not putting on the market. One consideration is, of course, the economic factor. It's not good to glut the market with new goods before the old ones wear out. Another factor, however, is the people's readiness. Company policy makers may feel that the public is not ready for such and such a thing and must be educated first before accepting a new product. Prescinding from any judgment of taste or morals, it took time for the manufacturer to put full colored ads of toilet tissue into popular magazines. The public had to be softened up for the (now endless) bad breath ads and the like. Large corporations like RCA, General Motors, Bell Telephone have all kinds of fantastic gadgets ready for marketing—but not until both the economy and the public are ready for them. (This is the sort of things one sees at World Fairs.) Biology holds fantastic and indeed frightening possibilities. Reading books like *The Biological Time Bomb* can either put you in awe at what science can do or stun you into amazement.

Now the point is, that those on the inside, the initiated, know all these things. When the first video telephone is unveiled, the people at Bell won't be overawed or surprised. When any of these modern miracles come to the public's notice, only the uninitiated will be amazed and caught off guard. So it is with religion. Take what we spoke about in the very first chapter, the liturgy. You recall that we mentioned that for at least a hundred years, liturgical experimentation was going on. Early magazines like *Orate Frates* were telling all. Books like Clifford Howells' forerunner *Of Sacraments and Sacrifice* were being read avidly, but not by you!

The initiated were not overwhelmed at the Offertory procession. Those people who were had not continued their religious education. True, in the past four or five years there has been an avalanche of books with every new theology from God is Dead to God Isn't. No one could keep up with all of the genuine information much less with all of the religious nonsense. Still, Mr. Average Catholic has been guilty for not doing his homework, for not reading, for not getting guidance on what to read and what magazines to subscribe to. If he has been guilty of pulling a religious Rip Van Winkle he ought not be surprised to wake up and find a strange new world.

— 3 —

Secondly, you have to realize not only are we, the teachers, reclaiming and reexamining the past, but that you the taught are receiving the results of this second look. By way of example, we can take a look at some things that have a new slant today that would touch on one's practical life. In the chapter on the liturgy we touched on others such as the color for the funeral and the new Fifteenth Station. Here we can add a few more shifts of emphasis that will concern the Middle Catholic unless he has read and opened himself to current education. We could begin with something as innocuous as eating meat on Friday. It seems a little thing, but the new law has caused many an argument. Deep down even the older Catholic knew that this was a Church law; that is, it could be changed and even removed as sometimes happened on holidays that fell on a Friday. Yet, long tradition gave the Friday abstinence not only a special place in the mind of the Catholic but it also became a kind of external sign of being one. A Catholic was one who did not eat meat on Friday. Yet, in the course of time the real meaning of Friday non meat-eating became *only* a sign. By that we mean that the external became far more important than the inner appreciation of willingly giving up flesh meat on behalf of the One who gave up His flesh for our salvation that first Good Friday. Questions of just how many ounces constituted a mortal sin became prevalent and, distressingly, somebody answered them! Horror of even touching meat was in no way proportionate to the horror of discriminating against one's neighbor. Then too, there was something unnerving, if not ridiculous, about the notion that one could wind up for all eternity in the fires of hell along with murderers, adulterers and dope peddlers for eating a half of a hot dog. Anyway, the whole Friday-meat question became so overladen with legalisms, fears and disproportion that the bishops said in effect, "All right, forget it. That is, forget the sin problem. Don't eat meat on Friday, but do it out of love. If you're not motivated from love, then eat meat without sin."

This brings up the question, by the way, of how many Middle Catholics read the beautiful statement of the bishops on the Friday abstinence question. If they read it, they would have seen that the Friday abstinence still does hold—but it holds out of love not fear of sin. Here was a change. Those who said, "I don't care what the pope said, I'm not going to eat meat on Friday!", missed the whole point. They hardened into dogma what was only a practice and a pretty good one at that. They seemed almost disappointed that one less possibility of sin was missing. They felt cheated again that the present day Catholic could do without sin what was sin in his or her day. And this harkens back to "our" guilt and "our" short-sightedness in ever putting the burden of sin on such a practice to begin with. It says much for our getting our values confused.

Or, take Christian burial practices. It used to be (and somewhere still is) the practice in some places not to bury a non-Catholic spouse in the same cemetery with his partner or to bury him in unconsecrated ground in the same cemetery. Or, if they were buried together, in some instances a cement wall had to go between them! When you stop to think about this, you recognized the anomaly. Here's a couple that could live together and sleep in the same bed together, but not lie side by side in separate coffins! Like so many rules, things like this just spring up as a kind of part of the thinking of the times; upon a second examination, however, one sees how un-Christian such things can be—and how, therefore, they ought to be changed. Someone, of course, who experienced the former rule is going to be awfully hurt when someone benefits from a changed rule; which shows our basic un-Christianity: that we should be sad that someone else gained a more humane and loving benefit than ourselves. If we are to be annoyed at all, it should be against those people who made up the unkind rules in the name of religion to begin with.

Other examples of new approaches would be new concepts on sex, marriage and poverty. Principles can remain the same, applications and statements of them may vary as the context of an age varies. In the famous usury example, the Church condemned it, and rightly so, in a precapitalistic era where usury meant exploitation. As the context of society changed, so did the condemnation on usury. As money capital became a major factor of productivity, so lending at interest became a legitimate business. It's not that usury, once wrong is now right. That wasn't the principle. The principle was that man should not cheat and exploit his fellow man. It found an application in usury at one time of history and no application in capitalism at another time of history.

Poverty once meant giving up material possessions and living without too many goods. Poverty meant living frugally and not buying luxuries and sometimes necessities. Yet today Father Andrew Greeley can argue in his book *Life For A Wanderer* that poverty in the American context of today might mean the opposite; that buying things might help the economy more, that creating jobs might be more useful to the poor, that if everyone bought only necessities we might send the economy into a spin. In poverty it's not the possessions, their ownership or lack, that make a man a sinner. It's the spirit of using things to grow as a person, the spirit of ruling goods rather than the other way around. Poverty is not what one possesses: it is what one can let go of for the sake of the kingdom of God.

More personal things are being reconsidered in present day context such as love, sex and marriage. A re-examination of older varied traditions are being made; for example, the ancient Greek custom of granting a divorce under certain circumstances and a readiness to admit that our Western Catholic Church has always, from the beginning, granted divorces under special circumstances. The point is that we're in a new era. New applications have to be made of Christian principles; old applications, like usury, have to be forfeited. New attention must be given to some very old and valuable traditions in our Church that have been ignored as the one party-line approaches in theology and canon law became predominant. Again, the average middle American Catholic is experiencing the tension of being caught in between the recasting of the new and resurrection of the old.

— 4 —

There's one final related point to discuss in this chapter; the Generation Gap—although we will talk about the youth in another chapter. I think it was Father Patrick Peyton of the rosary fame who coined or at least made popular the slogan that "The family that prays together, stays together." That's fine. The only trouble now is that the family can't even pray together! And why? Because sixteen year old Sue doesn't "buy" the rosary anymore and nineteen year old Stephen refuses to be a slave to "set" formulas. And we're not even mentioning all of the traumas and near heart attacks caused by son or daughter, a senior in high school, or home from college on Christmas vacation, announcing that they don't believe in God anymore or find the Church "irrelevant." The homes where such announcements have been made are legion. And so, religion, which once, above all things, united families, now separates them.

And the parents get back to that old sense of being cheated—and betrayed. Why betrayed? Because Junior was saying that his prof (a priest) says that you don't have to go to church on Sunday if it really doesn't mean anything to you or that people shouldn't be running to confession so much or that if the experience is "meaningful" you may have premarital sex! And if you want a serio-comic picture of a real loser, picture the parent listening to all of this from a son she doesn't even recognize! He went away in September like a big edition of her little boy; now, there he is, looking like Karl Marx or Alfred Lord Tennyson with shaggy hair, dirty clothes and an obnoxious mustache.

Again, we will talk of the youth in another chapter. The point here is still the educational one. The sons or daughters of the Middle Catholic are being exposed to all of the "new" things with all of their excitement as well as foolishness. But if Mom and Dad closed the religious book twenty six years ago, the religious gap becomes a chasm. Mom and Dad have not even kept up sufficiently with religious development to tell Junior where he's wrong (where he *is* wrong; he could be right, you know). Parents can only retreat with, "Well, that's the way I was taught!" The resulting confusion is the gap between those who know the old "one way" teaching and those who know variations on a religious theme. Undoubtedly one of the solutions for the generation gap, if it indeed does exist, is communication. But communication is possible only if certain basic terms are understood by both sides. Adults have a lot to offer and much of what they were taught is as valid and true today as when they learned it. This same old valid and true teaching may need a new dress, a restatement into the modern idiom, but this presupposes education and keeping up with things. For the Catholic willing to learn, we have listed in the appendix of this book a list of basic books. A little time with a few of them will be rewarding.

Was I taught wrong? Yes and No. Yes, perhaps in emphasis and restrictiveness; no, in the context of the past times and in the essence of the basic truths of Christianity. Love is still the measuring stick. Liberal or conservative, educated or uneducated, theologian and student will all ultimately be put to this measurement. If you as a person have been faithful to your convictions, have led a decent life, have repented and in general been a good person, then you're really not so far away, after all, from what religion is all about anyway.

CHAPTER VI

Bishops, Priests and Nuns

— 1 —

In their amusing and perceptive book, *The Peter Principle* the authors give guiding principles on why everything goes wrong. The main law is that in a hierarchical system every employee "tends to rise to his level of incompetence." By that the authors mean that a man may be quite able in his present job, in fact, so able that he is promoted to a higher position. But this new position with its larger responsibilities and extraneous duties is often too much for the newly promoted. Yet there he stays permanently incompetent in a position which is a step beyond his true competency. So rigid is this "law" that, according to the authors, there are no exceptions. Even the "Super-Incompetent" person comes under this law by getting kicked upstairs to an equally unimportant position (the "Percussive Sublimation") or by continuously moving sidewards into a series of multiplied positions (the "Lateral Arabesque"). As for the "Super-Competent" person, he so upsets the system that he not only does not win promotion because he won't conform, but is often dismissed. To many people (especially the liberals) this is an accurate picture of the Catholic hierarchy.

They argue that the bishops of this country, as in most others, have evolved in a rather closed system.

They usually are chancery workers, office men or rectors of seminaries. The majority of them have been to Rome to study. They reached the office of bishop precisely because of these connections. In turn, they will continue the in-breeding because, as it stands now, every present bishop sends in three names of episcopal candidates to Rome where bishops are chosen. It is obvious that a bishop will send in the names of those he can trust, those who have probably worked closely with him and thus who are similarly office-bound and, by presumption, equally out of touch with the people.

What happens next? Well, able as these men may have been in their office jobs, they succumb to the Peter Principle by reaching their level of incompetence as bishops because there's much more to being spiritual Father to a whole diocese than in teaching a philosophy class to (formerly) docile seminarians in a safe and secure routine. Moreover because the bishop usually is so far remote from his people any mistakes are not obvious and, besides, he has many levels of subordinates to hide his blunders. A bishop may turn out to be incompetent in an obviously public way, but this is not likely since he is a bright person, having been chosen because he went to Rome, and only those go to Rome who are the better students. The only thing that is likely to upset a well entrenched bishop is the "Super-Competent" priest who won't conform. He is usually buried in some small parish or is forced to drop out of the ministry.

About a half dozen years ago, writing in the now defunct *Saturday Evening Post*, Edward Sheehan described the typical American bishop and his relationship to the people:

> The American bishop is usually remote from his people, especially in the large urban dioceses; he lacks the

sense of community which the bishops of early Christendom shared with their flocks—but perhaps that is the price of modern progress. In many dioceses throughout the nation one is impressed by the big-business atmosphere in the chanceries where the bishops maintain their offices. Switchboards, receptionists and wall-to wall carpeting abound; electric typewriters and adding machines converse in pious whispers; the bishops manage their sacred corporations amid air conditioning and expensive walnut paneling. A California pastor suggests that the motto of the American bishops might be, "When in doubt, build." Their "preoccupation with brick and mortar," he says, "is essentially a release from frustration. They are confused by the complex challenges to faith in our society, and they hope they can somehow overcome the challenges by throwing up more buildings."

Festooned in the purple of royalty, genuflected to whenever he extends his bejeweled hand, addressed as "Your Excellency" even by unbelievers, it is not always easy for a bishop to sustain his sense of human frailty. Like the large corporation executive he so often is, the bishop sometimes withdraws into a world all his own, isolated from dissent by aids too awed by his apostolic charism to talk back. "We priests often fail to tell the truth to our bishops," says Monsignor Egan of Chicago, "We fail to give them the unpleasant information they need to make right decisions."

This, then, is the picture of the average American bishop: pleasant, intelligent, personable—yet the product and victim of a closed inbred, hierarchial system where, true to the Peter Principle, he quickly reaches his level of incompetence. Since leadership by definition means seeing and acting beyond the system it should be obvious why there are no genuine leaders in the hierarchy.

But let's backtrack a minute. This portrait may puzzle the Middle Catholic or upset him as being disrespectful to our bishops (and the priests and nuns will fare no better). But it is worth investigating this alarm, this personal uncomfortableness. The root of it is *distance*. Unless one has some relative in religion he has never had close experiences with priests and sisters and especially bishops. His contact with the bishop has been through the diocesan paper and on the occasion of the confirmations every few years. He was taught to respect the clergy and that their personal idiosyncrasies in no way detracted from them as personal emissaries of God and dispensers of His graces through the sacraments.

I recall a story my mother told me about her old-world father. When she was little someone had made a slighting remark about some priest. Incensed, her deeply religious father told (as was his wont) this story. Jesus and the Apostles were tired and thirsty after a long, hot day. As they were walking along complaining about the hot weather, they came across a crystal, clear stream of sparkling water. They all bent down and refreshed their thirst. Then they followed the stream, turned the corner and lo and behold they stopped in sudden shock. The clear and sparkling stream of water was coming out of a dead dog's head! Well (getting back to grandpop), the application was as clear as that water in the story. The priest is God's specially chosen one and his personal defects do not matter; he's still up on the pedestal as God's servant and the dispenser of graces. This story sums up the old attitude to the priest and religious and bishops. It sums up the "image," to use a Madison avenue word, that he has had. Most people know only the image. A lady once remarked to me that she didn't know how human priests were until she saw the movie *The Cardinal* on TV.

Because of the distance at times between the image and the reality, and because the system encouraged this arrangement, the average Catholic is both surprised and annoyed to hear criticisms of his clergy, bishops or priests; and yet they are human. Not in the sense that they have faults and shortcomings—the average Catholic always suspected that even if he didn't vocalize it—but human in the sense that they can be shaped by a system. They can be molded by a system and become closed in by a system that eventually puts them out of contact with reality. Such a schooling makes them not only dedicated to the continuance of the system they know but threatened by any indications of its demise. Hence Sheehan's description. The result is today the American bishops have been caught short with renewal and are finding it hard, after many years in a closed clerical society, to break out into the open arena of communication. Many are making heroic efforts with priests councils and people's councils, etc.—but this only points up the gap that has existed for so long. But, to average Catholics, bishops are a rare breed apart. Priests they know more about.

— 2 —

Or do they? Do they know what goes on in a rectory, what system molded them as seminarians, what room for creative growth they have? Perhaps no one has described the priest's position in the system better than the prolific Father Andrew Greeley. In his book *The Hesitant Pilgrim* he writes of the pastor-curate relationship realistically and accurately:

> The pastor enjoys nearly absolute power; there are precious few checks on his authority. . . . In any conflicts with his assistants, they will be transferred, not he. It is most unlikely that he will be removed, no matter

what he does. . . . The American pastor thinks of himself as primarily an administrator; it is as an administrator that he behaves and it is as an administrator that he will be judged by those whose judgment is important. . . . He is highly complimented when his people describe him as a "good business man. . . ."

Because his concerns are so heavily administrative and his curates have no administrative concerns at all, it follows that pastor and curates will have very different goals in mind. The curates usually will spend more time with people—especially the younger people—will be closer to the people, and more sympathetic to what the people want and need. . . .

In such a situation, the curate often moves in a very different world from that of his pastor, and the pastor finds himself increasingly threatened by the assistants who are a mystery to him. . . . It is but an easy step for a pastor to become suspicious of his assistants, to mistrust them, to supervise them as stringently as possible and to attempt to isolate them from the people as much as he can. . . .

Since he cannot trust his assistants, and cannot be certain of what is going on in the parish, a pastor may turn to someone else with whom he can share his problems . . . It may be a relative who lives in the house (to the acute embarrassment of the curates), or a trusted janitor or secretary, or head usher, or officer of a parish society. . . .

The pastor has all power and responsibility; the assistant has none of either. His work is liable to be at the mercy of one anonymous letter writer, or one chronic complainer, or one "spy" who rushed to the pastor with a story about what the assistant has done. Mother Superior, housekeepers, janitors are hard to come by, but to get another assistant is the easiest thing in the world.

In some supposedly "good" assignments, an assistant (even if he is over forty) must explain why he was not at a meal, where he will be when he does go out at night and to whom he was speaking in the rectory parlor. He must ask permission to go out of the rectory and is forbidden to talk to the people of the parish after Mass on Sunday. . . .

When one man has no power in a relationship and another man has all the power, it is almost inevitable that the relationship will be a poor one. . . .

The assistant further realizes that he has no "right of appeal." While complaints in an impossible situation may be sympathetically listened to and he will be transferred out of the situation, the assistant knows that almost any difference will be settled in the pastor's favor. . . .

There are many different ways a man can react to the discovery that he and everything he does are expendable. Some priests engage (if the pastor will let them) in work beyond the parish where their zeal and creativity can find an outlet free from pastoral restrictions. . . .

Add to this description the fact that the Roman Catholic Church is about the only large organization in the world today to operate strictly on the seniority system and it is obvious what further frustration is likely to exist in the priesthood. As one priest remarked, "There is something enervating about a setup where, to reach the top, one has only to fulfill the simple expediency of breathing longer than someone else." Merit does not promote rank in the priesthood and unusual initiative and talent threaten the whole system.

There is much truth to the latter remark. Creative priests often find it hard to function in a strict system. As we shall see below, the priest is called upon by Vatican II to be more active and more creative than ever, especially in the field of social work. If, however, a particular priest would like to heed that call, but is bound in a rigid system such as Father Greeley described, he will begin to feel tension; from tension it is a short step to frustration and from prolonged frustration it is a short step for some to leave the ministry altogether. Cardinal John Wright is one who believes that frustration is the chief cause. Some priests feel that they are blocked from experimentation, from new forms of ministry; they feel they are bound to old and meaningless forms of acting. In fact, many of those priests who leave immediately get into social work where they feel they can really help people without being bound by endless rules and ecclesiastical red tape. Books like John O'Brien's *Why Priests Leave* give many instances of this.

No one knows exactly how many priests and sisters have left. One Vatican official estimates that there are at least 10,000 requests on file from priests asking to be dispensed from their vows. There are thousands more who have left without asking at all. In the United States there exists an organization called Bearings which helps former priests and sisters to find their way back to the secular world. Among those leaving have been some of the most creative and energetic priests such as Charles Davis, famed Jesuit theologian Bernard Cooke and Jesuit philosopher Robert Johann.

How many of the laity are familiar with these situations and attitudes or even suspected them? Who among the people ever suspected such a closed system from the bishops on down that stifled men and led some of them to defection and alcoholism? This sort of thing has been brewing for hundreds of years and as the closed system became more closed, free associations and more liberal ideas became ever more suspect and many good men were forced out of the ranks. Much of the reaction to this system took root about seventy or eighty years ago in what is known as the Modernist movement where men like Tyrrell and Von Hugel and Cardinal Newman ("Super-Competents") wanted to let in truths from other sources and examine new ideas in the Church but were either forced out of the church or into disgrace. And yet, though some of the modernists went to excess and fell into heresy, the very issues which these men raised and were condemned for were accepted and promulgated by the Second Vatican Council!

In our own day, the lid has blown off and the public, unprepared for the destruction of the clerical image, has been scandalized. Books like the frenetic and juvenile *A Modern Priest Looks At His Outdated Church* caused a big uproar and was on the best seller list. In it Father Kavanagh, now Mr. Kavanagh, inveighed against legalism and impersonalization of the Church, the worst features embodied in the priests he knew as a boy. He cries out:

> There is no place for person in our Church. There is only room for groups that nod in blind assent. . . .
>
> The heroes of my work were the priests and sisters, more important than doctors or presidents, more wise than scholars or diplomats, more worthy of respect than police or even parents. Their decisions were clear and final, and could invade every facet of my life. When I was caught kissing with seventh grade passion I was solemnly turned over to the priest. When I skipped school, I was sent to the enraged pastor. In my school, Lincoln's birthday was outranked by the pastor's own. I greeted the priest each time he passed. . . . I could not criticize his sermons, question his actions, nor even mention his name without charity or praise. If he drank and showed the effects, he obviously had

a cold. If he snarled about sex or money, he was nervous and working too hard. I was not to talk back; I was to be grateful for criticisms, and never to refuse the most impossible request.

I hate the legalism of my Church. I hate what it has done to Catholics and what it has done to me. . . .

In many ways he railed against the narrow minded Catholic, the indifference of the parishes to the real needs of the people and excessive legalism in the Church. His book may have shocked some and indeed it is intemperate and petulant—yet it was read avidly by many and many people in the clerical state rejoiced that they had found a spokesman.

Then there was the revelation of Vatican II where some 2300 bishops from all over the world met at Rome in what was presumed to be a united and conventional shoring up of the party line. Suddenly the average Catholic found out from a determined press and books like those put out by the pseudonymous Xavier Rynne that there was deep and long standing divisions. No, more; there were deep and divisive arguments, a tremendous unleashing of what was apparently long standing problems and need for reform. The one-party monolithic image was forever shattered. Following such revelations, it was but a natural step that the lesser clergy should feel free enough to join in the shouting and in the creating of renewal. This, basically, is the occasion for much of the clerical static that has gone on in the past years and will likely continue. But, note, Vatican II's open dissension among the hierarchy was only the occasion. The cause lay elsewhere.

Some causes we mentioned already: the very inequality of the pastor-curate relationship, the suppression of creativity, the stifling effect of a strict seniority system, the catering to a kind of perpetual adolescence, the lack of permission to experiment and so on. But other factors are evident. First of all, priests and sisters are bona fide members of this generation. They, like all other Americans, have been brought up on hot dogs and coke and TV and the Beatles. They did not mature in a vacuum. Being thus of this generation they share its strengths, weaknesses and aspirations. They will be affected by peace movements, they have in their hands the documents of Vatican II with all of its new directions and they are quick to shuck off the old system and "get with it" in bringing about renewal. If they ape some of the present day slogans and postures this is not to be wondered at.

More basically, however, the present priests and sisters are products of a new wave of social consciousness. We have alluded to this before and will dwell on it more fully in another chapter, but here we simply stress the fact that Vatican II discovered new insights into the Church and new insights into the Church's social mission. Thus in the document "The Church in the Modern World", the council fathers say such things as this:

> Never has the human race enjoyed such an abundance of wealth, resources, and economic power. Yet a huge proportion of the world's citizens is still tormented by hunger and poverty . . . (art. 4).

> Every day human interdependence grows more tightly drawn and spreads by degrees all over the world. As a result the common good, that is, the sum of those conditions of social life which allow social groups and their individual members relatively thorough and ready access to their own fulfillment, today takes on an increasingly universal complexion and consequently involves rights and duties with respect to the whole human race. Each social group must take account of

the needs and legitimate aspirations of other groups, and even of the general welfare of the entire human family (art. 26).

This council exhorted Christians, as citizens of two cities, to strive to discharge their duties conscientiously and in response to the gospel spirit. They are mistaken who, knowing that we have here no abiding city but seek one which is to come, think that they may therefore shirk their earthly responsibilities (art. 43).

The possibility now exists of liberating most men from the misery of ignorance. Hence it is a duty most befitting our times that men, especially Christians, should work strenuously on behalf of certain decisions which must be made in the economic and political fields (art. 60).

With such exhortations from their own church, plus the whole renewed social consciousness of the times, it is no wonder that priests and sisters have wished to respond. The problem came (and still persists) that the Church had not only developed new means of social expression for the cleric and the laymen but felt threatened when new means were demanded. And where they were not forthcoming, some priests and sisters, with the documents of Vatican II under their arms, either struck out on their own or joined up with secular causes.

Thus an early case was Father William Dubay who publicly called for the removal of his superior (then Cardinal McIntyre of Los Angeles) for being behind the times. He even wanted to start a priest's union to bargain for better terms and "due process." Father Dubay is now married, Cardinal McIntyre has retired and many dioceses have, as a matter of fact, instituted due procedures whereby a priest can get a hearing for legitimate grievances with his superiors. (That there was no such machinery in practice is a commentary in itself.)

"Hot" names like Berrigan and Groppi make issues of war and social justice and housing. Some big names like the well thought of Charles Davis, the English theologian, left the Church and got married, finding the Church too inhuman and stated his case in his book, *A Matter of Conscience*. Others joined Martin Luther King, Jr., in his drive against racism. New social causes, dear to the hearts of the American boy and girl—now as priest and nun—have captured their imagination and they feel they are witnessing for Christ on the picket lines. The friction, as we said above, is that the "estabishment" the hierarchy, was caught short, felt threatened and is only now beginning to see the need to change some structures so that priests and nuns can have the creative freedom they need to survive as persons.

— 3 —

Much that we have said about the priest's condition applies to the nun's as well, but even more so. She had the least freedom to be herself. Father Robert Gleason, S.J., in his book aptly entitled *The Restless Religious* puts the case briefly when he says:

> Religious today claim that they are not leaving religious life because it is difficult or sacrificial; they are leaving because they are frustrated. They consider themselves betrayed as human beings in the intellectual order, the spiritual order, and the psychological order (p. 64).

Again, the general public never had any idea of any sisterly frustration. They looked at the nuns, admired them, as most people, Catholic and non-Catholic do—

and held them in high esteem. They were considered persons of great personal sacrifice and of wonderful dignity. They were ladies. The grief behind the convent walls for some (naturally not for all) was never aired in public, nor should it have been; but it was there. Personal initiative was stifled and the sisters were regimented in the novitiate and almost completely at the mercy of their convent superiors. They were given second class educations, picking up degrees during their many decades of teaching. They were bound to rules, mostly made up by men. Now, the sisters too have become influenced not only by Vatican II but, by the fact that they are children of their times and part of a Now generation. One sister sociologist put it this way:

> . . . There are two cultures coexisting side by side in American life. One is family-centered, traditional, stable, sheltered, relatively changeless, often rural, proud. The other is technical, swift, mobile, faceless, pragmatic, restless, pluralistic, urban. The question the sisters ask is, "Can our life retain its values in the new culture?"

Another nun comments:

> They (the new postulates) come with their guitars. They are full of joy and vivacity. The only Church they know is the Church of the Second Vatican Council, Pope John's Church: critical, questioning, free. But in our community the women training these girls are very rigid personalities and the new girls strike deadly fear into their hearts—they'll never fit into slots. These girls are reading Sartre and don't know if they still have faith, but the novice mistress makes fifty of them sit in a classroom for an hour after Mass because on the way to church one girl almost stepped on a worm and those behind her giggled. Another girl is told she doesn't have a vocation because she tidied up her room in five

minutes, when the rule said fifteen, and sat reading Albert Camus for the extra time.

A book published in 1967 is called *The New Nuns* and is a compilation of essays written for the most part by the nuns themselves and was the outcome of a symposium on that topic. A partial listing of the table of contents gives a clue to the rethinking about the religious life:

The Meaning of Virginity
Can Sisters be Relevant?
Nuns in Ordinary Clothes
Protest Movements and Convent Life
Freud and Sisters
Freedom of Expression in the Church
Nuns in the Inner City
Religious Communities in a Changing World

Not all the sisters, of course, want change, but many do. Many have had it with repression and the lack of the freedom to be themselves. They may want community life, but they want it with their personalities intact and with the possibility for personal growth. Those who don't find these qualities in convent life are leaving. They want participation in the creation of a better world. They too, are caught up in the new emphasis on social responsibility.

Again, the average Catholic saw only the facade. He saw not only those sisters who were genuinely balanced and happy, but he saw all of the sweetened manifestations in movies and TV. Ingrid Bergman in *The Bells of St. Mary's*, Loretta Young in *Come To The Stable* and Sally Field as *The Flying Nun* were delightful people who warmed our hearts, but they were not real. They were more caricatures. There were other less happy sisters and situations which were repressed and hidden from public view. Nor is it likely that a public, long conditioned to the fantasy of the perfect nun in the wrinkle free habit, would or could accept any other image.

— 4 —

If the priests and nuns, taking their cue from Vatican II, have entered the mainstream of social reform; if they, taking their cue from a new secular culture, have been speaking out more and experimenting with new forms of ministries and living; if, taking their cue from the general unrest of the church and society, they have been making a case for optional celibacy—they have also been guilty of the concommitment excesses. In other words, if the lid is taken off a formerly repressive and unilateral authoritarian system, there will be a reaction. Some priests and sisters, having already been retarded at the juvenile level by their early clerical training, have responded like juveniles no matter what their age. They have shot off into excessive reactions like a teen-ager with his first car. Like some of the liturgy, they have immediately tied themselves to the present culture which becomes notoriously out of date as last week's best selling record. In the throes of post-conciliar confusion they don't know how to respond in a mature way. The priest-sociologist Andrew Greeley writing in the January, 1970, issue of *The Critic* puts it this way:

> Catholicism is burdened with a substantial number of clergy and religious whose emotional maturation was aborted in their late teens by the seminary and novitiate experience. The fixation of their emotions in late adolescence was not a complete disaster as long as the rigidly structured Church sustained their personalities.

But many of the rigid structures have been swept away by the Vatican Council's renewal program, with the result that the Church suddenly finds itself with a considerable number of professional personnel who are, psychologically speaking, still very much adolescent. It is not dysfunctional to be psychologically adolescent when you are chronologically adolescent, but to be psychologically adolescent when you are chronologically adult can be intolerable. Many of our adolescent clergy and religious cannot tolerate complexity or ambiguity. They seek simple solutions, magic answers, instant competence and overnight maturity. There is little in the way of firm inner-core to their personality, and not much in the way of convictions or commitments to shore them up. The romanticism that is surging across the country is just what they're looking for.

There are other anomalies that go with the confusion of renewal: nuns getting out of uniform and into lay dress so that people can't identify them as nuns at the precise time in our culture when everyone else is getting *into* uniform. There are nuns who want to be exactly the same as other people so as not to frighten them off. Yet they are doing this at the precise time when the youth (who are usually their targets) will face them with long, wild hair, shaggy moustache and beard, bell bottom trousers, Indian head band and psychedelic clothes and fully expect these nuns (or any adult for that matter) to accept them as they are as persons. They fully expect the adults to look right through any outrageous packaging to them as people of dignity, meaning and esteem. In fact, some youth will purposely dress in an outrageous manner to *force* others to learn to disregard externals and to accept them as persons. The irony is that they (the youth) are quite willing to give this same acceptance to adults on the same terms—even to nuns in medieval garb. Those nuns so anxious to divest themselves of such garb have missed the point of the youth rebellion.

Then there are the cultural talking clergymen doing their own secular thing in a world in which many of the youth have turned to mysticism. They, too, may have missed the point of the youth rebellion. Other clerical by-products are our T-shirt Mass-saying priests offering Mass before an underground of hippies all, of course, in their own "vestments." The picture is not unlike one of those Sullivan cartoons where two hippies with all of their paraphernalia of dress, posters and drugs are laying on their pads and one says to the other, "I used to be a Catholic, but I couldn't stand all that weird superstitious stuff."

In a former age it was the delight of seminarians to point at the anti-intellectualism of the *Imitation of Christ* where it says, "I would rather feel compunction than know its definition." Today, they agree with that statement as a wave of new anti-intellectualism sweeps the country in reaction to the strict and rigid scholasticisms of a former day. As in the liturgy, busyness seems to be the order of the day for some priests and nuns. They are anxious to find Christ in the slums, Christ in the market place, Christ in the ghettos, etc. As one balanced priest whose duty it is to run seminaries has commented, "all this is fine, but you sometimes suspect that they should try finding Christ in Christ."

The Middle Catholic is rightly disturbed by rumblings in the ranks of the clergy and religious. He is apt to feel a combination of embarrassment and anger. Acknowledging that there are some clergy and religious who, as we just indicated above, are immature and juvenile, still we must rejoice at the fact that the others are agonizing over Christian concerns. They may be confused, may want a period to rethink their commitment, but committed they are. If they are impatient with slow-moving Mother Church, the impatience is often on behalf of the people whom they want desperately to help. Our clerical crisis is not, as in the days of old, one of indifference, one of greed, one of ignorance; no, our crisis is one of love, the desire to serve with the Church or, alas, without it. But to serve, to be someone, to be free to grow into true apostleship—the Middle Catholic must believe that this is truly the case for so many. The Middle Catholic has the right to feel disturbed but he should also realize that the whole clerical fuss, rightly or wrongly handled, is about Christian commitment; and if the nation's 170,000 sisters are going through turmoil, if the clergy is reexamining its ministry and its precise identity, these things are a sign of a new vitality coming, a transition to a new world, a new rededication to witnessing for Christ.

CHAPTER VII

The Youth

— 1 —

A chapter on the youth in a book concerning renewal in the Church is justified if for no other reason than the youth represents all that is obnoxious about renewal to many Middle Catholics. The youth tend to be renewal's loudest practitioners and most fervent advocates. In fact, to the average Catholic, some of the renewal activities of the youth come very close to revolution. Besides, it is the youth who are most likely carrying the protest banners, strumming the guitars at the folk Mass, leading the impromptu prayers, quoting from Berrigan or Marcuse at Epistle time and advocating what appears to be free love and a structureless religion. Most Middle Catholics are openly or secretly threatened by the youth. In or out of the sanctuary, in or out of the Church, they don't understand them. Moreover, getting back to renewal in the Church, many of the Catholic youths of today have never consciously known the period before renewal. They are its heirs and, as the future majority (as we shall see below) of the country, they will take renewal where they will. It behooves us, therefore, to look at the youth situation in general and some local domestic Catholic problems in particular.

> I see no hope for the future of our people if they are
> dependent on the frivolous youth of today, for certainly

all youth are reckless beyond words . . . When I was a boy, we were taught to be discreet and respectful of others, but the present youth are exceptionally wise and impatient of restraint.

Our youth have an insatiable desire for wealth; they have bad manners and atrocious customs regarding dressing and their hair and what garments or shoes they wear.

Perhaps it's not exactly fair to start this chapter on youth with complaints from parents; yet, on the other hand, it takes some of the sting out of the present urgent situation to realize that the first quotation was written by Hesiod in the eighth century before Christ and the second one was written by Plato three hundred years before the Christian era. It seems that, whatever the slogan of the times, there's always been a generation gap. From the time when Julius Caesar offended the Senate with his crazy togas and mod hair cut, from the times of the young upstart Alexander the Great who managed to be the first world conqueror, from the time Romeo and Juliet had parental problems, the gap has been there. What is so different about today?

The difference is numbers. The difference is communication. Professors of sociology tell us that those under twenty five make up almost half of the U.S. population and this ratio will increase on the side of the youth. The difference is that this is the generation brought up on TV and instant worldwide communication which has made them, not citizens of this or that town or country, but citizens of the globe. The difference is that society has so changed that teen-age has replaced adolescence. A few years ago a sociologist Edgar Friedenberg had a book significantly entitled *The Vanishing Adolescent*. Once more we must look at society today as contrasted to that of seventy years ago. At that time, we recall, few people went to school. It was a rural society and the family was held together emotionally and financially very tightly since each depended on the other for economic stability and survival. Everyone from Grandpop to Junior had to work on the farm. The work may have been hard and often monotonous and boring and sometimes unrewarding, but such early, well-defined chore work had one important benefit to the adolescent and preadolescent: it gave him a sense of self identity and self-worth. He knew what he was and what he was going to be, he had no "identity crisis" so popular with the college class today and had no vocational problem: he was going to be a farmer like his father before him and his father before him. Since he didn't need much schooling he could settle down to marriage and responsibility on a family scale. Adolescence was short—and then on to adult work and responsibility.

Today, all that has changed. Adolescence has become teen-age and this may extend, not to four or five years, but to fifteen. In a highly technical society as today, schooling becomes important and the adolescent may have to go many years. During this schooling time he has no economic use or function. He must stay at home and so remain dependent on his parents right up to his graduation from college. In the meantime, given his uselessness on the labor market and his long-term education, what is he to do with his energies? Society symbolically drugs him—and at times, actually. He is given many possessions and money; he becomes such an economic money spender that if all the teenagers were to stop tomorrow they would send the national economy into a tailspin. He is distracted with fads, over organized and kept busy. Such a routine may keep him occupied but it may have the side effect of perpetuating his adolescence and retarding his identity.

Lacking the security of self-identity, the adolescents must identify with the group more and more. In the book *The Adolescent Experience* the authors say:

> Adolescence is disappearing as the period in which the individual can achieve a decisive articulation of the self. Nowadays the youngster merely undergoes puberty and simulates maturity. If this amiable but colorless form of adolescence is indeed a new thing in our country, then we would have to single out as one important reason the extraordinary extenuation of today's adolescence. Given the long preparation required for advanced technical training, given the uselessness of the adolescent in the labor market—parent and child settle down for a long, long period of time during which the child will, in one way or another, remain a dependent being: . . . Nowadays the adolescent and his parents are both made captive by their mutual knowledge of the adolescent's dependency. They are locked in a room with no exit and they make the best of it by an unconscious agreement by which the adolescent forfeits his adolescence, and instead becomes a teenager. He keeps the peace by muting his natural rebelliousness through transforming it into structured and defined techniques for getting on people's nerves. The passions, and restlessness, the vivacity of adolescence are partly strangled, and partly drained off in the mixed childishness and false adulthood of the adolescent teen culture.

With such a useless role for the adolescents in today's society, they frequently grow up without responsibility (and this is not always to their liking). Add to this permissive upbringing of some parents and a rebellious generation should be a surprise to no one.

More. Add to the youth's confusion other dramatic

changes in society. For one thing, the breakdown in family life patterns. In 1969 there were some 680,000 divorces. The children of these divorces are bound to feel some effects. Materialistic parents who are on the go leave a communications barrier intact. Absentee fathers, either through divorce or extended trips or commuting, has had its effects on the childrens' lives even academically. In the *Saturday Review* Dr. Urie Bronenbrenner cites the influence of father absenteeism:

> Some relevant studies have been carried out in our own society. For example, I, with others, have done research on a sample of American adolescents from middle-class families. We found that children who reported their parents away from home during long periods of time rated significantly lower on such characteristics as responsibility and leadership. Perhaps because it was more pronounced, absence of the father was more critical than that of the mother, particularly in its effects on boys. Similar results have been reported in studies of the effect of father absence among soldiers' families during World War II, in homes of Norwegian sailors and whalers, and in Negro households with missing fathers, both in the West Indies and the United States. In general, father absence contributes to low motivation for achievement, inability to defer immediate for later gratification, low self-esteem, susceptibility to group influence and juvenile delinquency. All of these effects are much more marked for boys than for girls.

Surveys consistently show that adolescents view parents as the most significant figures in their lives. Yet suburban living often means that father gets home after the children are in bed. If mother works there's no mother to come home to after school. Family life and intimacy do not exist for many adolescents. They do have a desire to communicate with someone and eventually they either begin to go around with transistors glued to their ears or become more dependent on the gang or peer group for acceptance and identification.

Add to all these things the fact that the glacier of tradition is breaking up. All the old standbys seem to be losing their force: organized religion, family life, patriotism. Values are shifting at the precise time when half the nations's population is coming of age. The result of all this leisure and material possessions is frequently one of rebellion on the part of some youth. They really don't like what they call our modern materialism and our (the adults) preoccupation with it. When wealthy kids dress up in rags or refuse to bathe they are saying something about adults who put such a premium on deodorants and smelling nice that they spend billions of dollars a year advertising this good news. They don't like the impersonalization of society, where zip codes abound, area codes are necessary and numbers are increasingly replacing faces. From being "Detached Americans" as one Philadelphia TV station called us, they react as flower children with love for everyone.

They don't like the rat race they see their parents running and themselves running. They don't relish a job for a job's sake; they are asking for personal fulfillment. They are sophisticated and weaned on TV, know more about the world at five than their parents at twenty-five. The world has shown them that there are different peoples from Americans, different customs, different political, religious and sexual mores. The TV, money and mobility put the adolescents in instant contact electronically all over the world. They know there are different ways of doing things.

Being citizens of one world, having leisure time to be

critical, it is but an easy step for the youth to enter politics, to form student groups, to declare that any racism or divisions among men in a world united by instant communication and the common fear of the nuclear bomb is an anachronism. It is but an easy step to shake up the splintered and localized world of the adults. Thus students confront authority, rail against their "corrupt" society and affect brotherhood. They are impatient with a former morality that was restrictive and preoccupied with sin rather than love. They deplore a morality that was so self-conscious and not at all social conscious. They suspect a religion that could preach about the terrible sin of eating meat on a Friday but not say a word about the gross sin of prejudice, racism and the killing of six million Jews. They rebel against a religion that represses the outspoken, censors the books and forgets the impoverished. They reject a religion that is uptight about sex and teaches a Catholic form of Puritanism.

Thus, they have turned eagerly to Church revival and to secular protest, confrontation, hippiedom, and drugs. Thus they look in esoteric bypaths for meaning to life, for direction in a time of change, for substance on which to build a better society. They preach love, flower power, freedom, brotherhood and tolerance. Whether they're right in all of this is another question. And, as an afterthought, it is hardly needful to add that the youth's activities and prolonged teen-age state have been helped to survive comfortably by unscrupulous adults who provide the drugs, the pornography and the fads and thus treat the youth for what they really are to them: a highly profitable and marketable item to be exploited.

– 2 –

The youth are, of course, not above criticism. There is a suspicion for instance, that some youth rebellion is not principle as much as background. If some of these youth are from broken homes and from insecure backgrounds, is their activity political or psychological? Is each protestor a leader? Does each activist see the principles involved? For every genuine leader, how many are merely hangers-on? Surveys show that the high percentage of drug users and sexually promiscuous are unhappy within themselves. They are hurting on the inside and taking it out on society in general. How many of the look-alike, listen-alike, feel-alike, talk-alike youth are leaders? How many do their own thinking? How many swallow slogans whole?

The college activists often fight hard for tolerance and brotherhood. Often they themselves won't give the others the same privilege. Witness the boorishness of those students who booed and catcalled men like Galbraith, Humphrey and others who went to speak on the college campuses. They were prevented from speaking by the very ones who advocate free speech.

The youth by nature see things in black and white. The older generation has made mistakes, but it has done some good. It has put up the schools and orphanages and hospitals. There are millions of husbands and wives who do love each other and take care of their children. There are adults who are concerned. The overt protesting activist adolescent is in the minority in life if he is in the majority in the headlines.

Some youth are naive if they think that mere slogans like "Make love not War" and "Peace" and so forth will of themselves bring about improvement. There's a lot of simple nitty-gritty living that takes a great deal of patience and tolerance and the capacity to defer immediate gratifications for later goals; the youth don't always show these qualities. A psychoanalyst like Dr. Bruno Bettelheim blames much of the student rebellion on parents: he sees the unwashed and unkempt youngster as the one practically scrubbed out of existence by his mother in the name of good hygiene and loving care; he says these kids' intellect was developed at an early age but at the expense of their emotional development and thus they are still having temper tantrums; the political efforts betray the wish that the parents should have been strong in their convictions; big students who invade deans' offices and sit in his chair are fulfilling the little boy's wish to sit in papa's big chair; overpermissive parents and overextended adolescence—all are factors, he believes, for the confused and militant youth.

Still, there's more to it than that. Adults must realize what a different world it is today. Change is the hallmark in every place and in every study and in every direction whatever. Church renewal in every department—liturgy, faith or morals—is but one phase of change that the youth have grown up with. They have never known anything but change and many of their religious postures, so upsetting to adults, are but phases of this fact. Besides, as children of the space age they are embarking into territories where previous experience is no help. Adults must begin to appreciate what Dr. Margaret Mead so aptly pointed out in the *Saturday Review* (January 10, 1970). There she emphasizes once more the differences of the world today, that we are in a new era and a new age where both adults and children are strange and where past experience is not valid anymore. She writes:

> For the first time human beings throughout the world, in their information about and responses to one another, have become a community that is united by shared knowledge and danger. As far as we know, no such single, interacting community has existed within archaeological time. . . .

> The younger generation, however . . . are like the first generation born in a new country. They are at home in this time. Satellites are familiar in their skies. They have never known a time when war did not threaten annihilation. When they are given the facts, they can understand immediately that continued pollution of the air and water and soil will soon make the planet uninhabitable and that it will be impossible to feed an indefinitely expanding world population. . . .

> . . . They live in a world in which events are presented to them in all their complex immediacy. In their eyes the killing of an enemy is not qualitatively different from the murder of a neighbor. They cannot reconcile our efforts to save our own children with our readiness to destroy the children of others with naplam. They know that the people of one nation alone cannot save their own children; each holds the responsibility for all others' children. . . .

> . . . Like the first generation born in a new country, they listen only half-comprehensibly to their parents' talk about the past. For as the children of pioneers had no access to the landscapers whose memories could still move their parents to tears, the young today cannot share their parents' responses to events that deeply moved them in the past. . . .

> Today, nowhere in the world are there elders who know what the children know. . . . In the past there were always some elders who knew more than any children

in terms of their experience of having grown up within
a cultural system. Today there are none. It is not only
that parents are no longer guides, but there are no
guides. . . . There are no elders who know what those
who have been reared within the last twenty years
know about the world into which they have been born.

This, then, is the youth of today: citizens of a new
one-world planet whose space age technology makes it
impossible for the adults raised in another society to be
of an immediate practical guide. They can only perform
that most saving and valuable function of teaching their
children how to learn (not necessarily what to learn),
how to be committed and how to hold onto and extend
their Christian values system in a new era.

— 3 —

The purpose of this chapter is to give the reader some
understanding of the formation of the youth of today
and at least try to see the origins of his own perplexity
and the frustration of the adult world in trying to cope
with them. Within this context, we can take a look at
some of the practical problems the Catholic parent is
likely to encounter with his offspring in upper high
school and college—problems parents are apt to interpret as direct results of renewal.

One of the first frictions may be the Catholic parents
versus the "new" teaching their children are receiving.
We covered most of this ground in Chapter V. There we
mentioned that much that is "new" is not really so; it is
more apt to be ancient, but from another tradition. The
trouble was that only one scholastic tradition gained the
upperhand and, unfortunately, became the Church's
"official" expression of truth. In fact, often the truth and

the doctrine became identified with the Thomastic terms that embodied it. Now the kids are learning other rich traditions, traditions which often do not coincide with their parents' religious upbringing and education. Secondly, we must concede that some progress has been made in psychology and in the educative process in the past decades. Some of the religious teaching is being presented in a format and a style and in a multi-media dependency that was not the "in" thing forty years ago. Whether these pedagogical ventures are the best, time will tell but at least some of the new presentations are trying to build on what the other social sciences have taught us; they are trying to present the eternal truths in the form and in the relevancy of the day and for that they should get an "A."

On the other hand, the new religious presentation and, we might add, the new religious teachers, are not above reproach. As with the liturgy, the religious doctrine may be so tied down to the current culture that it runs the danger of forever becoming obsolete and thus not sustaining. Also, it is interesting to note that some of the new teachers present the class in the spirit of new religious freedom, but often cancel out that very freedom by being so doctrinaire themselves. If they smirk at the rigidity and intolerance of the past ages, some of them are equally intolerant of what has been good in the past and is still very much valid. Sometimes the new religion teacher delights in shocking the students when he glibly tells them that there was no Adam or Eve or scoffs at the apple-temptation story or such, but puts nothing in the place of the vacuum he's created, except, perhaps, student cynicism. Perhaps the most devastating criticisms of some religion teachers is their lack of scholarship. They simply repeat the high-flown theories they heard in college, pass off as the right answer the most casual speculation of some theologian and are not really well grounded themselves in theology. Humility, scholarship and dialogue would go a long way in helping the parents in the "new truths versus the old truths" situation that disturbs many Catholic households.

Another trauma for the Catholic parent is the announcement by Junior or Sis that they're not going to church. The homes today where such a problem exists are legion. "My daughter doesn't want to go to Mass anymore." "My son says Mass is not meaningful, so why should he go? That's what's wrong with these kids. Everything has to be 'meaningful' today." "My son always went to Mass until he went to Catholic high school. Don't they teach that anymore?" Such statements are frequently on the lips of many parents today. What about such statements? Are the kids dropping off from Mass attendance? What's the story behind all this?

First of all, there are no reliable figures on how many adolescents are staying away from Mass on Sundays. The only thing we can say is that there seems to be some degree of slippage and that statements, anxiety about Mass-going and parental resentment over the failure of their children to go are indications that the phenomenon exists. One thing we must not examine for an answer is the rhetoric which blames all of this on some conspiracy of the liberals in the Church who never teach God's law anymore or some new breed priest or sister who preach to the adolescents that everything must be free and spontaneous and meaningful. Nor do we have to listen especially to the over-sophisticates who think that all this is great, that the kids are "telling us something," that the kids are helping to destroy an old corrupt system anyway. No, we must look elsewhere; and "elsewhere" is something we've alluded to before in this book and will speak of again: the immigrant Church in America and its response to a hostile majority culture.

Recall that in chapter III we indicated that we Catholic Americans were a minority group in a hostile anti-Catholic Protestant country. Discrimination against Catholics ran high forcing them to draw more tightly together and making them reaffirm their Catholicism all the more earnestly and emphatically. Not yet accepted in the mainstream of American life, still considered foreigners, American Catholics tended to be super-Catholics and super-patriots. (cf. early American bishops like Carroll, England, Keane, Spalding) Even long after the barriers began to break down our ethnic protective atmosphere clung. Only the symbolic act of John F. Kennedy's being elected President officially put aside the foreign image of the American Catholic. But until that time he tended to find support from his own group, from some "anti" group as opposed to the dominant hostile group of the time. Thus we saw that the American Catholic founded his own newspapers in opposition to an unfair, Protestant-dominated press. He established his own parochial schools in opposition to a Protestant-dominated educational system. He founded the Knights of Columbus as a counterpart to the hostile Masonic orders. In other words, when the Protestant nativists were running rampart, cohesion among the Catholic minority group became extremely strong. Novena-going, rosary-saying, forty hours, routine in morning prayers, Easter duty, reciting the Angelus three times daily—all these things provided a definable framework of identity and security for the Catholic sub-group.

Sunday Mass attendance fell into this category as well. Going to Mass on Sunday was not only a truly religious act, but it was also definitely a part of the "counter-culture" of American Catholicism. In other words there was an unrecognized sociological undercurrent supporting Sunday Mass attendance and the other religious routines. There was a subconscious need and urging to be faithful. However, on the other hand, when such subconscious elements began to disappear then a shift in performance could be expected. For example, we know that Knights of Columbus and Sodality meetings were better attended yesterday than today. This fall off is not for mainly religious reasons, but for sociological ones. It's just not as necessary today to prove one's Catholicism by being a Knight. As a part of America's life, a Catholic can join the Kiwanis or Elks. Social needs can now be fulfilled everywhere and so the necessity for an identifying "in" group becomes less compelling. So it is with Mass attendance. Going to church on Sunday was not solely, of course, a social thing, but such faithful attendance was definitely supported by such subconscious elements as we have described. Or, in other words, Mass attendance on Sundays in the 1970's has to be motivated for more purely religious reasons than ever before.

So, back to the adolescent. If he stops attending Mass regularly on Sundays it may reflect the fact that he is a child of the common culture. He is not fighting for Catholic acceptance, he is not seeking identity and recognition from a dominant other culture. He *is* that culture and so the subconscious pressure on him to identify himself as a Catholic by going to Church on Sunday is simply not there. Secondly, the adolescent is more openly secular today and his culture is more global and scientific and he is frankly not completely orientated to established religious values. Thirdly, the adolescent is less susceptible (for better or worse) to all authority and to old traditional rituals. Every ad on TV tells him to "get with it" and "do your own thing" and "think young" and to "come alive." His whole conditioning has taught him to seek the novel and new. He feels no predisposed allegiance to the old or traditional. He thus tends to be more rebellious and more experimental and his thoughts about Sunday Mass surely will come under this general impulse.

Does this mean to say that we should just ignore our sons' and daughters' announcement that they find Mass "irrelevant" or "not meaningful"? No, what has been written here is merely to demonstrate that the adolescents are children of their times and their church attendance habits need not necessarily mark them out as less religious but only as less inclined to traditional forms, less compelled to rely on routine, less quick to accept a ritual because it's always been done that way and less susceptible to thinking sin is involved in missing Mass because they consider theirs to be an honorable conscience following its own dictates and integrity. What has been written implies that other approaches might be helpful.

Such as? Well, such as approaching the adolescent with an open mind procedure. It is doubtful that any teacher should merely tell a sixteen year old adolescent that he or she need not go to Mass if he or she doesn't find it meaningful, period. That's hardly the final word for an immature, searching mind. The same teacher would not tell his sixteen year old son who decided to drop out of school or get married that it is solely a matter of what he thinks. There would be some dialogue, some recognition that older, more experienced minds might have something to offer by way of consideration. So too, with Mass attendance. The teacher or parent should at least offer dialogue and considerations which urge the adolescent to keep an open mind and not make a final serious decision at sixteen or eighteen.

What considerations might be offered? The consideration of community for one thing. The young people are highly concerned with brotherhood. They are highly social conscious and know that they are their brother's keepers. They recognize that no man is an island, including themselves, as they move daily in constant social relationships, attending sit-ins and pep rallies even when they have a headache. Community is man's hallmark and religion is no exception. No matter how far back the archeologists dig and search they always come up with some Temple or assembly hall indicating man's constant propensity to gather together to worship the deity. This reflects that man, the social being, must be social even in his approach to God. The community would be strange to be so social in everything else whatever and suddenly so totally private and isolationist in its approach to the Almighty. So, the community provides the temple, the church, the mosque and everyone goes there—even with his headache—realizing that he does not go to get anything out of it, but to give something to it, to add his presence to the sum total of the community's effort at worship. Indeed the word "liturgy" itself means the *public*, communal worship of God. Thus, for the adolescent, the challenge might be made in presenting him with what is essentially a choice between himself and the community. Just as he does go to the pep rally when he doesn't feel like it, so might he not consider joining the community worship since he is not an island—even a religious one? It might be suggested that if it comes to a toss up between staying in bed Sunday morning (especially a cold one) and joining the community at worship—even passively—that it might be better to make a mistake on the side of "otherness," the community. He might be reminded that we are already too conscious of our self indulgence and self deception. Error (in going to church) committed where others are concerned might be preferable to error (in staying home) favoring oneself. And thus the adolescent might be urged to favor going to Mass while the Sunday attendance matter is still up in the air.

Another consideration for the adolescent might be to ask whether this action of staying home will truly make him grow, bring him closer to God, make him more Christ-like. In other words, such serious decisions must be weighed in favor of improvement; that one truly becomes a better person by staying home, that one spends his time in reading or meditation or prayer, that one grows spiritually as a result of his decision.

A final consideration might be to look at the liturgy itself. Perhaps a more meaningful liturgy geared to the adolescent might be an answer on the part of the parish or the Church at large. Where such meaningful liturgies have been tried, Mass attendance among the adolescents has improved.

Again, the older generation person might be impatient with all of this. It will be easier to exclaim to the adolescent, "Listen, young man, as long as you live under this roof you'll go to church with the rest of us, and that's that!" And this may be a good approach, especially for the adolescent who is testing his parents values rather than defying them. Still, there must be the understanding that there is a different mentality today, a different culture and that the framework of spiritual reference for the adolescent is often different. The whole question of adolescent Mass attendance may not be a liberal plot to drown the kids in an ocean of freedom (yes, there are liberal excesses) but the beginning of a more sincere church-going adult of the future. Perhaps, as Father Karl Rahner suggests, Christianity will become a smaller, elite group of the future and that those who participate in the sacred Mass liturgy will be there because they want to be there and neither the fear of sin nor the subconscious pressures of subculture cohesion will be the motivating force, but rather dedication and love will be. A naive hope, perhaps, but the risks involved in freedom are always naive.

A final point of parent-adolescent religious conflict might be the area of morals, particularly sexual morals. In the age of penicillin and contraceptives when the triple threat of infection, detection and conception is no longer real, the kids may again feel that if a relationship is "meaningful" (that word again!) then premarital sex is justified. More than anything else this subject is likely to make the average Catholic parent see red. Again, the answer is not to thrust a simple "It's a sin!" attitude on the kids, but to try to reach them on their own ground. Their own ground these days is personalism; that is, regard for the person and a highly individual and personal relationship ethics. The trick is to help the youth see that some sexual activities, in the long run, are not truly loving. The average parent may neither know this approach nor, very likely believe in it. Here the parent needs help and a few good books are his best ally. I would recommend the very fine paperback *But Don't*

You Really Love Me? by Father Joseph Champlin (Ave Maria Press), *Sex, Love and the Person* for the college student by Peter Bertocci (Sheed & Ward) and, for the boys, the author's *A Boy's Sex Life* (Fides Publishers.)

Most of the youth, it seems, are basically conservative. Even those who may be considered "far out" are looking for substance to life and even for God. Among some college students there is a large interest in Oriental religions, Pentecostal sects and basic fundamentalist biblical theology. Many use in an informal way religious symbols. They are searching. In any case, the youth want a relevant religion and they will shortly be a majority in the Catholic Church. Their general liking for any church renewal is both the extension of their own youthfulness and the reflection of their status as citizens of a new world. They deserve adults' friendship and communication. Adults should at least talk with them and listen to them. What we have written in this chapter about the formative influences on the youth, about the fact that they have entered into a wholly new world should be considered again. They have been raised in fantastic scientific discovery, they have never known the United States not in a war, they saw the first men on the moon and they expect and will get even more scientific wonders and changes in the future. In that sense their cry "the future is now" has some meaning. We adults cannot always give the answers and perhaps not even the questions, but we can give the experience of living, the wisdom of a quieter approach of life and, above all, a deep faith in the Father of the Universe.

CHAPTER VIII

Sex, Sin & School

– 1 –

There are few things in this age of Church renewal that upset Catholics, and especially Catholic parents, more than the Three S's: Sex, Sin and School. There is the on-going controversy in the schools' sex education program; there are new concepts of sin and confession leaving one with the impression that what was formerly sinful is now positively virtuous; finally, there are the attacks on the Catholic school system, not by outsiders, but from within the ranks itself. If this is what is meant by "renewal," some Catholics want no part of it. In our continuing effort at understanding, let us in this chapter examine these three problem areas.

Many people are upset about the possibilities of sex education in their schools, both public and parochial. It seems that sacred sex is going to be another classroom subject at best and a how-to-do-it routine at worst. People have strong feelings about this. They are apt to say, "Sex education belongs in the home. There's already too much sex around anyway; everywhere you look, in the movies, TV and books and magazines. We're a society that is drowning in a sea of pornography, nudity and perversions. Let's not bring all these things into school."

Such concerns have reached the shouting and organizing stage. Persons worried that sex education in the schools is unhealthy and that it will eventually undermine an already over-exposed group and usurp the rightful duties of the parents—such persons have banded together into highly vocal groups campaigning against any form of sex education. There are now several national organizations of this type: SOS (Sanity on Sex), CHIDE (Committee to Halt Indoctrination and Demoralization in Education), POSSE (Parents Opposed to Sex and Sensitivity Education) and PAUSE (People Against Unconstitutional Sex Education). In addition to these parent-orientated organizations, two major groups have joined the ranks: The Christian Crusade founded by Billy James Hargin in 1947 and the John Birch Society. The Christian Crusade is concerned with secularism and feels that replacing God and the Bible with sex education has not been a gain. The John Birch Society sees sex education as part of a communist plot to sap the moral fiber of the nation's youth.

Some Catholic parents who sympathize with these organizations are dismayed that the public school obsession with sex education has infected the parochial school system as more and more Catholic schools are going in for it. Renewal in the liturgy is one thing; teaching the kids sex in the fifth grade at St. Luke's school is another. Let us clear the air and see the pros and cons of sex education.

The first and most basic misunderstanding about sex education is that very phrase itself which is a most unfortunate one. It definitely connotes a teaching about how to have sexual intercourse and where babies come from. Actually, such information is but a minor part of what is called sex education. In fact the phrase "character education" would be a more appropriate and a more accurate phrase for that is what genuine sex education is about.

Genuine sex education is about character, about what it means to be a person, about what it means to be male and female. It is about masculinity and femininity. It is about family life and personal relationships. In fact, family life is one of the foundations for proper sex education. A good sex education course builds on family life and tries to unfold the vision of one as male and female in that relationship. It tries to get the child to accept himself as male or female for no person is just a person: he or she is a masculine or feminine person. The child can never act except as a male or female with his or her own pecular vision, shape, attitudes and values. Sex education teaches them to be human, to have values, to respect others and to know themselves.

Within this general framework of teaching a child how to be the male or female person he or she is, there will naturally be introduced the facts of human reproduction and the related topics of human relationships from dating to marriage. But these facts are not shown by themselves but within the context of being a person and respecting the other and not exploiting another human being. Reproduction information is given as one and only one factor making up the boy or girls' total Christian value system. Perhaps a few quotations from the Interfaith Statement on Sex Education representing the Catholics, Protestants and Jews, will be helpful:

> Human sexuality is a gift of God, to be accepted with thanksgiving and used with reverence and joy. It is more than a mechanical instinct. Its many dimensions are intertwined with the total personality and character of the individual. Sex is a dynamic urge or power, arising from ones' basic maleness or femaleness, and having complex physical, psychological and social dimensions. . . . Responsibility for sex education belongs primarily to the child's parents or guardians. A home

permeated by justice and love is the seedbed of sound sexual development among all family members. . . . We recognize that some parents desire supplementary assistance from church or synagogue and from other agencies. . . . For those who would introduce sex education into schools, however, the question of values and norms for behavior is a problem—indeed, the most difficult problem. It is important that sex education not be reduced to the mere communication of information. Rather, this significant area of experience should be placed in a setting where rich human personal and spiritual values can illuminate it and give it meaning.

In Chicago, a comprehensive sex education program has been introduced into many of the Catholic schools covering grades from first to eighth. Significantly the series is called "Becoming a Person" and works closely with the home in bringing about the development of the child's personality. There are five basic themes in this series. They are:

1. The Family. The importance of parents, responsibilities to family, family roles, etc.
2. Understanding Yourself—self insight and acceptance of self as a worthwhile person.
3. Maturity. Life, growth and psychosexual development.
4. Relating to Others. Respect for person, understanding differences, cooperation, communication.
5. Values. The social and psychological basis for ethical and religious values, rules, self-discipline, service, love, etc.

This gives an idea of what sex education is really about: a program of helping the child to become fully the male or female person that he or she is. A minimal of time we repeat is spent on reproduction, but necessary time; most of the time is spent on self acceptance and maturing as a human being—becoming a person.

Are there reasons for such a course? There are. Some obvious reasons are that there is so much sick sex around, so much pornography, so many negative attitudes about sex that it behooves the adult world who are interested to reach the kids first with the truth and the beauty and the dignity. Times *are* different. When most adults today were children there wasn't too much overt sex around at least in the form of paperbacks and movies and such. There was an atmosphere of restraint, of privacy. Most people grew up in stable neighborhoods and witnessed stable marriages. In this sense, they received a wonderful context. Today, with open sexual activity and innuendoes, broken homes and mobile families and customs, this context is absent. Sex education, in its best meaning, recognizes this situation and is trying to fill the gap.

Secondly, basic sex education is given in the home whether the parents know it or not: they give it negatively or positively depending on how *they* relate to each other in their masculine and feminine roles, on how they accept themselves as man or woman, on a display of the obviously affectionate bond of marriage—but, often parents need extra help. They cannot always cope with the vast amount of antisex that the children get in the streets or in school. Besides, it's difficult for most parents to discuss the subject with their children, and many don't. The results have often been disastrous. In his delightful book *Our Bed Is Flourishing* Dr. Robert McCready says:

> Since the 1930's, society has moved fast and very far. Many of the older generation do not like some of the things that are happening today; but we should never

forget that the impetus for all this change came from mankind's desire to improve, not only his own condition, but, especially, his children's welfare. We started on this road because we believe that in a free society the only way to regulate behavior is to provide all the facts which will help people make informed, intelligent decisions. Some of our present difficulty may be blamed on our lack of decision. We have not gone far enough in providing education, particularly in the sexual field. Now we are confronted by the old dilemma of too little knowledge too late to be of value. We reiterate the claim that sex education is best conducted by the parents in the home. On paper, this is excellent theory. In practice, and in the quiet security of my office, sixty percent of my patients admit to having inadequate knowledge for their own sex lives; and they do not feel at all competent to provide it for their children. Time and again, workers in the fields of sociology and psychology are showing that such education is not being given in the home. Perhaps it is time we admit that most parents do not feel capable of giving their children sex education, or they are reluctant to carry out their obligation for other reasons (p. 6).

The document from Vatican II on Christian Education says that "As they advance in years, they should be given positive and prudent sexual education," but if the parents don't do this, who will? The answer is, of course, the "street" and the professional pornographers will gladly and, for a fee, supply the lies. It seems that truth given first and joyfully, is the best defense.

But there are genuine problems in sex education. For one thing, not every teacher is qualified to teach it and this goes for priests and sisters. A teacher must have grasped his or her own sexuality for it is attitudes more than facts that will impress. Teachers need to be trained and need to be comfortable people in this field. Secondly—and this is the major problem as the Interfaith statement points out—there is the question of morals and the question of right and wrong. Can the teacher in the public school project no moral tone or not answer what will necessarily be ethical questions? What about the norms of sexual behavior? In a pluralistic public school system, one code cannot be preferred over another. A real fear of the future is that some ultra parent who believes in free love and who is anxious for his son or daughter to experience "meaningful" intercourse as soon as possible will object to *any* ethical suggestion on such questions. Will the school be able to resist his demands for *no* moral tone? Is the school prepared for a court case test which will be resolved in such a parent's favor? Will the built-in tendency to the lowest common denominator bring sex education down to a social health program with no ethical overtones whatever lest such would offend a professed atheist or advocate of free love?

Christmas carols with religious orientation are out of the public school system now; so is public prayer and, in some recent cases, saluting the American flag for those who opt not to. The same fate may well await any ethical suggestions in the matter of sex. It would seem that an out and out partisan approach might be the best. Perhaps a solution would be to take advantage of released time or inviting the different clergymen representing the different faiths to come in to field the moral questions for their respective groups. In the parochial school system, Catholic or Protestant, at least a definite moral code can be given in the matter of sexual behavior. Hopefully, this will be a positive and joyful approach, free of the Puritanism and sin-mentality of the past.

A final problem in sex education either in the public

reaction against a too strict mechanical approach to it previously. Heretofore there was a large emphasis on the objective sin; that is, such and such a thing, if done, was a sin. True, we always knew that for sin one had to have knowledge and consent, but these elements somehow lost their position and force and the result was people all over the country confessing as sins what were in fact non-sins. For example the lady who confesses missing Mass because she was sick is still at an infantile "taboo" level. There couldn't be sin without her consent. She could not help it if she was sick. She did something wrong by not going to church, but not every wrong is a sin and never will be a sin until we look at the person involved and their knowledge and their consent. Because instances like this multiplied, a reaction has set in trying to see as sinful only those things truly perceived as such by the living and acting person. The switch has gone from the thing to the person. Morality accordingly is undergoing a new look and taking a "look-at-the-person" approach.

It must be admitted that in the past, Catholics were brought up on a negative sin mentality. Sin was multiplied all over the place and made so pervasive for every little thing that it brought Catholicism into ridicule. In an instance we mentioned previously a man could be condemned to hell forever for eating three ounces of meat on a Friday and find himself in that same hell with some underworld figure who corrupts thousands by selling dope or trafficking in prostitution or murder. Somehow this didn't seem equitable. The minute prescriptions covering Catholic life and the sacraments, often with penalties of sin, have produced guilt-ridden and scrupulous Catholics. Jaroslav Pelikan, a friendly critic of Catholicism and himself a Lutheran minister, noted this in his book on the Church called *The Riddle of Roman Catholicism.* He cites cases in Catholic journals where questions like this would be asked:

> Question: "Is there any reason to fear that lip-stick will break the eucharistic fast?"
>
> Answer: ". . . It is not conformable with theological teaching to warn women against the use of lip-stick before receiving Holy Communion on the ground that they are likely to break their fast."
>
> Question: "If the lips of a woman who is receiving Extreme Unction are coated with lip-stick, is there any danger that the anointing of the mouth will not be valid?"
>
> Answer: "If there is a thick coating of lip-stick on the lips, there would be grave danger that the anointing of the mouth performed on the lips would not be valid; and in that event the validity of the sacrament would be doubtful. . . ." (p. 87)

With such moral considerations given to such detail and minutiae and even the doubt that a sacrament took place, it is no wonder that a moral system would have to be renewed. Obviously there are weightier things to be discussed. The new emphasis on what really is a sin and social problems reflect a more realistic approach to the world and its problems. Sin is still in, but as a reality that concerns human beings, not make-believe cases where sin could be incurred almost unknowingly like some tribal taboo.

Morality is further undergoing an emphasis in the area of social consciousness. Formerly sins were all concentrated on private ones that an individual could do against God. Little was really taught in respect to justice to all men; that racism might be a particularly unjust violation of charity; that antisemitism was not the spirit of Christ; that poverty and hunger ought not to exist in the land of plenty. With the new one-world reality of today we are now aware that what happens in one part of the globe not only is instantly communicated to another part, but that that other part is also affected by it. We are our global brothers' keepers but unfortunately, our pat moral teaching has neglected to develop and expand this attitude. Morality today is concentrating on the social aspect of Christianity.

Along with the social consciousness there has arisen new forms of communal confessions. Generally these communal confessions are private confessions as of old simply put into a ceremonial surrounding with others. Usually there are a group of people who proceed into church singing a song; there are common prayers and litanies, private confessions, but public absolution and the public recitation of the penance. Roots for this sort of thing go back a long time and the social aspect of penance has a venerable history. Again, the average Catholic not knowing his church history does not realize that the confessional box goes back only four or five hundred years; that no children's confessions were heard up to the eighth or ninth century; that at one time there were three sins—idolatry, adultry and murder—that could be forgiven only once and once only. No second chances were permitted for these sins; that confession was received only once and at the hours of death. A good run down on the new approaches to confession is the author's book *It Is The Lord!* (Fides Publishers).

Childrens' confessions are undergoing changes because of the new insights that psychology has offered us, especially with the work of such famous men like the Swiss psychologist Piget. It is now determined that children cannot have the necessary insight for sin until a much older age, around twelve or thirteen. They can do naughty things all right and they can know they're doing them, but the wider concept and the rational concept of sin and the heavenly Father is simply beyond their capacity. Since they really cannot commit insightful sin until early adolescence, it would seem wiser to postpone their first confessions to a time later than seven years old.

Conscience is another misunderstood and misused cry today. Again, especially the young upset their elders when they cry, "But if I think it's all right, it's all right." Or, "I don't have to go to confession unless I think I committed a sin"—and he or she hasn't gone in almost a year, clean contrary to the earlier upbringing of their parents. There have been abuses in the past where Catholics were almost told that their consciences did not count; what mattered was what the Church or the priest told them. So pervasive was this attitude that in frequent cases people, over the most minor case, would run to the priest either out or inside of the confessional to ask his advice or obtain his pronouncement. On the other hand, in reaction to this sort of thing, people today are making up their own minds. Unfortunately, this sometimes amounts to whim and they do not realize that following one's conscience is a false premise unless it is an *informed* conscience requiring the same integrity and inquiry as any other intellectually honest stance. Prayer and consultation are still prerequisites for the formation of conscience, not spur of the moment "inspiration" or feeling.

The formation of the consciences of the young is of vast importance and mistakes have been made, especially in the area of sex. Accusing a small child of impurity is putting an adult mind into a child's head. Shouting "dirty" or "nasty" to the four year old who is being concerned with his or another's sexual organs is to give panic and guilt preconditioning which will plague that child all his life long. Modern day morality, for all of its excesses, is at least trying to get the relationship off the mechanical rule plane to one of a personal matter with a Father Who loves. Person-to-person morality, the "I—Thou" relationship is reasserting itself in place of a less satisfactory legal mentality. This, basically is what is happening in the area of sin and morality.

— 3 —

At the end of the 1960's it was obvious that Catholic schools were in deep trouble. This trouble, on the surface, revolved around one point: finances. School systems like the famous free parochial system in Philadelphia began charging tuition for the first time in its history. Cincinnati dropped the first three grades in the Catholic schools. Teachers were unionizing; schools, grammar and high, were closing for lack of funds. If this weren't bad enough certain Catholics were questioning the Catholic school system itself. In the spirit of renewal, in the spirit of generally questioning every former tradition, some people had doubts about parochial schools. Too ghettoized, they said; or too inferior to the public schools; too partisan; too embracing in the sense of taking so much time, money and personnel from other worth-while apostolic ventures.

Still, with all of these criticisms, and with the genuine financial crisis that the school in the 1970's face, the average Catholic and the above average Catholic wants their parochial school to remain. In December, 1969, the

National Council of Catholic Men publicized the results of a survey concerning Catholic education taken among what they called the "elite" of the laity. Overwhelmingly the survey opted for Catholic schools. And, yet, there was one large contradiction to this desire: they were not sure how and if they wanted to support them financially or morally! In other words, there was such a wide variety of feelings about funding the schools, about the priorities they should envisage that no one over-all feeling emerged. And this is the real issue.

The financial crisis, although genuine, is but a surface problem. The basic problem is that a common agreement and a common basis for supporting the Catholic schools has vanished. To appreciate this, we must recall once more, our early history in this country. Catholics were immigrants in a hostile country. We saw several times how they huddled together for protection, for security and for identity. They could at least find a definition as a people, as a religious class, in their own sections of town, in their own parish churches. Why not extend their position in society by building their own schools? This was an attractive idea since, as we have also seen before, the public schools were so often Protestant rooted and anti-Catholic orientated. The building of the schools was a great stroke of genius as most people admit today. The schools did provide a vehicle for Catholics to make the transition from their old alien status to educated citizens of this country. It also helped to support their own identity as Catholics in a pluralistic society.

It is probably difficult for the average American Catholic today to appreciate how necessary it was for the early Catholics in this country to have schools and parishes so that they could hold on to and be themselves.

They were really not accepted in society at large; they had no face in a Protestant environment. But in their homes, their parishes and, most of all, in their schools, their need to be someone was fulfilled. In short, there was a general need here and this need *provided a broad agreement* for the erection of the Catholic school system. Our grandparents were happy to sacrifice to put these schools up to maintain the Catholic identity. Today, this broad agreement no longer exists and this is the dilemma of the Catholic schools.

Why? What happened to this general agreement? Basically what happened was that the Catholic school system was successful! It produced educated people. The old prejudices died down, affluence arrived, the desire for more and better education arose and a new sense of social consciousness budded forth. The very Catholics who were educated in the system began to question it vis-a-vis other priorities: should so much time and money go into such a small proportion of the Catholic school population and so little into the larger majority now in the public schools? Should so much be spent on, say, eight hundred children in St. Mary's grammar school and so little by comparison on the fifteen hundred children in CCD? Since education was valuable, how did the parochial compare with the public schools? (The current assessment of the 50's was that the public schools were better academically.) Then, too, what about the poor and deprived? If schools put in tuition and then raised them, did this not out-price the underprivileged?

Such were the questionings of the parochial school educated adults. They all still felt that the parochial system was valid and had much to offer, but they were split on the subsidiary problems such as those listed above. This splitting of opinion, this difference of reassessment has splintered the Catholic adult population enough that no one common agreement exists on a national scale which would give spirit, elan and synthesis to maintaining the vigor of the parochial school system.

In short, the spirit of renewal, of seeing old traditions in a new light, has split the votes; not indeed, as we have seen, as to whether Catholics want the parochial school system (they do and they do with emphasis) but as to where to put the priorities and how to make them more integrated into the over-all witnessing of the Catholic Church.

We have seen that the financial crisis caused by rising costs in construction, higher pay for the increasing number of lay teachers, etc., is not the major problem, but a serious one. At this writing, consideration is being given to Federal Aid to private schools. But even here there is a lack of a Catholic consensus. The National Association of Laymen in 1969 came out opposing any Federal aid to private schools and even indicating a sentiment in favor of phasing out parochial schools. In the light of the National Council of Catholic Men's survey the NAL does not really represent the mainstream of Catholics, but their dissent is once more symptomatic of the split of opinion about the system. The real villain seems to be Catholic apathy. There doesn't seem to exist the sheer determination to seek and obtain Federal money for the plight of the private school. But, once more, even this underlines the lack of agreement and a common national spirit among Catholics.

Catholic schools have performed noble service in the past. They are important as one authentic voice in a pluralistic society speaking to others. They are still near and dear to many Catholics who genuinely want them to stay in existence. Dissent about them is a direct outcome of renewal and the resulting increase of sensitivity to other arenas of action. But if they are to survive, more than nostalgia is needed. What is needed are Catholic men and women ready to put it on the line financially and morally for the Catholic school.

As each drew his sword
On the side of the Lord.

For over four centuries Protestants and Catholics have drawn their swords on the side of the Lord. Each side was absolutely convinced of its own righteousness and also of the crimes of those whom they called their "adversaries." Any relations between the Christian Churches were usually limited to controversies between their respective theologians.

While this was going on some Christians were thinking and reflecting about the words of Christ. The more they thought, the more they began to see the scandal of separation. Jesus' prayer was, "Father, that they may be one as we also are one, that the world may believe." They suddenly realized that it was the Christians themselves who were preventing the realization of that prayer. God has left us free to resist Him! A prayer of Christ is sterile because of us! And the rest of the world—the world of non-Christian and unbelievers—they look in amazement and incredulity. After all, they judge on what they see and they see a Christian world divided and they are not impressed. Well might they retort with the Christian saying, "Physician, heal thyself!"

As average Catholics, although we see the force of these thoughts, we are caught in an emotional bind. All our lives long we were taught not to fraternize with non-Catholics. We were forbidden to enter their churches, much less could we attend one of their religious services. We could not read their Bible, nor marry them without a dispensation. We could pray for them since they were plunged in darkness, although this was token since there was the vague feeling that most likely we would find no Protestants in heaven anyway. They had betrayed the Truth, led by a renegade priest Martin Luther.

Moreover, over the centuries, there were the mutual wars to add to mutual distrust. And there was prejudice and Catholics in the United States felt the brunt of it. From the beginning, American Catholics were to feel deep discrimination and practically all of their responses, as we have seen in past chapters, were a reaction to this: their (the Catholics) schools were founded because of the Protestant tone and outright anti-Catholicism of the Public school system of the time; their newspapers were established because Catholics could not get a fair hearing from the secular press and so on. Then there were other forms of bias. Catholics were forbidden to hold public office right up to the twentieth century. The campaign of Al Smith and John F. Kennedy showed how rampant anti-Catholicism was up till our own day. Only two colonies allowed Catholics in and gave them tolerance and Maryland was the only one to issue an Act of Tolerance. Even that, as John Tracy Ellis points out in his excellent and readable book *American Catholicism,* did not endure:

> In spite of this memorable action of Baron Baltimore's government, the effort proved in vain; for in the ensuing struggle the Puritan element overthrew the proprietors regime, and thereupon the assembly of October 1654, repealed the Act of Toleration and outlawed Catholics. Once in power, the Puritans wrecked a terrible vengeance on the Catholics by condemning ten of them to death, four of whom were executed, plundering the houses and estate of the Jesuits, and forcing the priests to flee in disguise into Virginia. It is true that Baltimore regained control for a few years, but the sequel to the "Glorious Revolution" of 1688 which had encompassed the downfall of King James II also deposed

the Catholic Calverts. . . . The Church of England was
established by law in 1692 and the Catholics were compelled to pay taxes for its support . . . (p. 27).

Again, in later times, the historian comments:

If in times of stress it is often difficult to maintain sincerity, as the actions of the Continental Congress dem-
onstrated, it is then just as difficult to adhere to old
prejudices and principles. General Washington—who
was personally free from religious prejudice—made
that evident to his troops encamped at Cambridge in
November, 1775, when he discovered that they were
once more preparing to burn the pope in effigy and insult the Catholics in the annual celebration of Guy
Fawkes Day. He put an end to the nonsense at once . . .
(p. 35).

Moving up to the 1800's we find the founding of *The
Protestant* an openly anti-Catholic newspaper. The
American Protestant Association (APA) was established on November 22, 1842 declaring that the principles of popery were "subversive of civil and religious
liberty" and that therefore citizens were uniting to defend Protestantism. Msgr. Ellis goes on:

The constant agitation of groups of this kind inflamed
the tempers of thousands of Americans who otherwise
would probably have remained at peace with their for-
eign-born and Catholic neighbors. It was not surprising
that violence ensued, as it did in August, 1834, when a
midnight mob incited by the harangues of the Rever-
end Lyman Beecher—burned the convent of the Ursu-
line Sisters at Charlestown, Massachusetts. Philadelphia rioters in May, 1844, were responsible for the
burning of two Catholic churches, the loss of thirteen
lives, and the wounding of many citizens (p. 63).

The existence of later organizations as the POAU (Protestants and Other Americans United) and the Know

Nothing groups all attested to the rampant anti-Catholicism. It wasn't until the election of the first Catholic President in the 1960's that this bigotry was officially laid to rest.

These historical elements are important background material if we are to understand the Catholic stance towards Protestants as we have inherited it in this country. *That stance was the natural and understandable one of defense.* The lines were drawn and so the walls of moral tariff went up high. Rules multiplied on the Catholic side in the form of such items as we mentioned above: all associations and fraternization on official levels with Protestants were forbidden; the rules concerning marriage, burials, taking part in their religious services etc., were many and precise. Everything was geared to keep the two bodies distinct. If Catholics were anti-American bound to the commands of a foreign ruler, then Protestants were heretics who, having left the true Church, were groping in the morass of moral and doctrinal decay. With such attitudes in the air, emotionalism ran high and, except for a few enlightened men on both sides, little was done to penetrate the barriers between the two Christian bodies.

What were these few enlightened men we sopke of discovering? Having set aside their personal prejudices, they were digging at theological roots and they were discovering that, in spite of the passionate rhetoric on both sides, there was, doctrinally, much in common. This was not to be entirely wondered at; after all, the roots of both sides were common ones. In fact, these men were finding out that there were more shared theological positions than differences; that there were many common traditions sacred to both sides even if the emphasis were different. Even the whole melee of the Reformation, they saw in later perspective, was really mixed up so much with politics that the genuine religious issues became muddied and almost peripheral. So they continued to study, to talk, to think and pray over the divisions of Christianity.

The first real break into communications between Catholics was, ironically, forced upon them during World War II. Although America remained untouched by the ravages of war, Europe did not. Its institutions were shattered. Terror and suffering and the basic struggle to survive threw together for the first time men of widely different religious convictions. Both Protestants and Catholics, fighting for survival either in war time jobs or in concentration camps, met and had the opportunity to exchange ideas. One problem, both found, was that their terminology and vocabulary were hindrances to dialogue. After all, each side was trained in terms familiar to itself; priests and ministers knew their own ecclesiastical wordings, but not those of the other side. Yet they wanted to talk about many things. So they began. The friendships and dialogues, started during those difficult war-torn years, persisted afterwards. Men met and continued to talk and learn about one another. This was the first opening.

The second opening was within the Catholic Church herself. By and by she began to shed her image as a triumphant, self righteous institution inherited from the Middle Ages and see herself as she really was: a Pilgrim Church, full of frail men, plodding along the path to salvation. Underneath all of the pomp and ceremony, underneath the high altars in marble and ermine wraps and bright red robes were human beings, redeemed by Christ and yet still capable of mistakes. In other words, the Church began to see herself as humble, in need of purification, a Pilgrim. Thus, with candor, at Vatican II, the Church in front of the whole world, said:

> From her very beginning there arose in this one and only Church of God certain rifts which the Apostle strongly censures as damnable. But in subsequent centuries more widespread disagreements appeared and quite large communities became separated from full communion with the Catholic Church—developments for which, at times, men of both sides were to blame.

Still more remarkable, the Church went on to say these bold words:

> St. John has testified, "If we say we have not sinned we make him a liar, and his word is not in us." This holds good for sins against unity. Thus in humble prayer, we beg pardon of God and of our separated brethren just as we forgive those who trespass against us.

In other words, the Church admitted that, as history shows, she was wrong at times in policies that unduly alienated others. She now knew that Christ summons her "to that continual reformation of which she always has need." With such pronouncements, ecumenism officially got off the ground.

Ecumenism is a dialogue among Christians. It is not meant that all Protestants should turn to Rome. Rather, ecumenism is geared that all Christian churches find unity *in Christ*. Ecumenism is looking closer at the common beliefs shared by all Christians. These common beliefs were always there but naturally got lost in the in-fighting struggles. Calling names and committing mutual persecutions is not the best climate to see where things were the same. We always shared many things: Scripture, for example; both sides have always believed in the Bible as the word of God and that is a very large point to share. We shared Baptism and confirmation, the belief in one God, the centrality of Christ, the redemption, the forgiveness of sins, even in some churches, devotion to the Blessed Virgin Mary. Luther, for example, not only repeated the traditional doctrines about Mary but defended them vigorously against her detractors. Ecumenism is looking at common grounds of belief. This is a necessary start if we are to make Christ's prayer a reality.

But good ecumenism is disagreement too. There are differences between Protestants and Catholics. There are even differences among the Protestant denominations themselves so it is hard to pinpoint them exactly. These disagreements do matter. "They do," as Robert McAfee Brown, an early pioneer in ecumenism, says, "or they could not have persisted for four hundred years." The Australian Bishop Brian Gallagher expressed the same thought, ". . . any unity of the churches achieved by bargaining, compromise or by soft-pedaling unresolved differences would be spurious. It is true that we cannot force one another to see the same truth, but we can love one another warmly, sincerely and unpatronizingly."

Dr. Brown himself finds three chief and deep differences between Catholics and Protestants. First, there is a difference on what authority means in both Churches, particularly the question of the infallibility of the pope. Secondly, he finds serious difficulties about the teachings on the Virgin Mary, especially with the Catholic doctrine of the Immaculate Conception and the Assumption. Thirdly, he notes the basic differences in the Protestant and Catholic understanding of the structure of the Church, especially the bishops' role. The Catholic believes that a definite form of structure is part of God's revelation—a concept presently being questioned by some Catholics and equally defended by Pope Paul. Protestants put less emphasis on the inviolability of any given form of structure.

Ecumenism is talking over the agreements and disagreements and making the efforts to put aside the nonessential rules that were emotionally motivated. So, these days a Protestant can be married at a Nuptial Mass with his minister present. Catholics on occasion can attend Protestant services. Both can have unity weeks of common prayer. These things, of course, disturb some Catholics, but on examination we find that the disturbance is an emotional one: so long defensively forbidden to associate in any way with Protestants such a Catholic finds unity moves bewildering. Yet if he realizes that the rules of the past were emotional reactions based on prejudice and fear on both sides, he should not have too much difficulty in seeing that, as those same prejudices and fears are removed, so too should the symtomatic rules.

But it is difficult for some especially on the everyday practical level. One woman said, "I don't know. When I go to bridge club all the women say to me, 'Ah, I see you're coming over to our side. You're becoming more like us everyday!' I don't know what to say." This, we grant, is hard to take for one who was schooled in the old separatist way. Evidently these women are not only referring to unity and dialogue affairs, but to more practical matters such as Catholics now singing in church (and Protestant hymns at that!), the lay reader and commentator and the erection of lay parish councils, etc. Still, such things are only returning to *our* original traditions. Singing is an old Catholic tradition ranging from the hymns of St. Ambrose in the fourth century to the Gregorian melodies in the Middle Ages, to the elaborate counterpoint harmonies of the eighteenth and nineteenth centuries. To pick up something we've always had but put aside (and one suspects, once more out of reaction) is not going Protestant. As to common ceremonies and church-going, again there must be a look at the basic point; if the worship is to God through Jesus Christ, it can't be wrong whether in a quonset hut, or a Protestant cathedral or a Catholic church. To meet in anyone's church around Christ and "with, in and through Him" to offer prayer can never be wrong. As Christ himself put it in the Gospel:

> John said to him, "Master, we saw a man driving out devils in your name, and *as he was not one of us*, we tried to stop him." Jesus said, "Do not stop him; no one who does a work of divine power in my name will be able in the same breath to speak evil of me. For he who is not against us is on our side." (Mark 9:38-40).

As in so many other things, as we have shown in this book, the underneath realities tend to be different from the emotional attachments or the emotional associations we made about them. Ecumenism is a case in point. Anyone who is upset that Protestant Christians and Catholic Christians cannot only pray together, but even borrow from each other common traditions that for one reason or another got submerged—such a person is reacting emotionally. More. Such a person is responsible for causing a prayer of Christ to remain unanswered. After all, we are *people* and all Christians are striving in Christ towards the Father so we can't be as different as all that. One is reminded of one of those delightful stories told so well by Joan Windham in her marvelous book, *Sixty Saints For Boys*. In the story about little St. Hugh she sets the scene thus:

Well, at that time the Christians and the Un-Christians were horrible to each other, specially the Un-Christians, so horrible that they lived in different parts of the Town; half for the Christians and half for the Un-Christians, so that they needn't see each other too much. They even had their own special shops and hotels, which was very silly because, after all, they were all *People* even if they were Un-Christians and Christians, so they weren't so different as all that (p. 335).

Not only are Catholics and Protestants people, but they have so much in common, they have so sprung from common apostolic origin that it would be a shame for them not to explore unity in a trustful and interested way.

A final comment surely should be this: today's world is a most complex one. Science is performing its miracles and creating its monsters. No longer is the world splintered but it is now bound together by common interests and common communications. Note how united the human race was on July 20, 1969 when every man, black and white, Protestant and Catholic, believer and unbeliever, rich and poor, Irish and English, Arab and Israelite—all men's eyes were on two human beings walking on the moon. How actual and how symbolic that things could never be the same now that that "giant step" was indeed taken for all of mankind. But not only does the human race have a common concern about space, but is now forever bound by instant mass communication and, more menacingly, bound together by fear of a bomb that can, at any moment, cause instant and world wide total destruction. Local problems have become a thing of the past. Division becomes a luxury we can no longer afford and disunity becomes as passé and as obsolete as racism. There are now larger problems facing

the human race that must be answered *by men of faith,*
united in a common cause; else the unbelievers will fill
the vacuum while the Christians fight. The whole concept of religion is at stake in today's world. John Cogley,
in the 1969 year's end issue in the *New York Times* put
it this way:

> The basic questions are concerned with whether Chris-
> tian belief and distinctive Christian communities can
> survive in an age shaped by the scientific mentality.

> With men reaching into space, will the idea of a tiny
> planet as the spiritual center of the universe and the
> beneficiary of a divine redemption lose all credibility?

> At a time when biologists are closer and closer to mas-
> tery over life and death, do such concepts as the 'soul'
> or a personal eternity make sense?

These are basic and frightening questions for all men
of good will, but especially for those who count themselves as followers of Christ. These questions are so profound that they demand the total resources of all men.
Such questions cannot tolerate division among those
men whose common faith in Jesus Christ must give
them the strength to answer them, a strength that comes
only from unity.

— 2 —

But what about the Jews and ecumenism? They are
not of the Christian community. What interest can they
and we have? First of all, the Jews would be interested
in Christian unity and inter-faith dialogue with Christians because they too would be alarmed at any head-
way of secularism against our common Jewish-Christian
traditions. Secondly, the Protestant-Catholic dialogue
is encouraging to Jews who wish to speak also with us;

for we must remember that our Christian heritage has Jewish roots. Israel of the past has had a definite role in God's plan; we all admit that. Moreover, the Jews have in common with us the Fatherhood of God and the sacred books and they can teach us a great deal about the social consciousness that they have always had. Finally, Jews themselves would be understandably interested in Christians becoming less antisemitic.

Christian antisemitism goes back to the first century, perhaps to Paul himself who, as a former Pharisee, took the role of a spurned lover and turned somewhat against his former religion. The decision at the first Council in Jerusalem to opt for a Universal Christianity instead of a purely Jewish type layed ground for division. The separatist attitudes of the early Christians, the counter-reaction fanaticism of the early Jews contributed also to Jewish-Christian mistrust. Future history accented the problem and anti-semitism in the Christian fold became a reality.

The very first ecumenical council at Nicea, for example, went to the trouble of fixing the Easter date independent of the day fixed by the Jewish Sanhedrin in Judea for the observance of the Passover. The prevailing mood was expressed by the Emperor Constantine himself when he declared, "It is unbecoming beyond measure that on the holiest of festivals we should follow the customs of the Jews. Henceforth let us have nothing in common with this odious people; our Savior has shown us another path. . . ." Pope Innocent III wrote to the French Count Nevers who had treated some Jews graciously, "They are under no circumstances to be protected by Christian princes but on the contrary to be condemned to serfdom . . . ." The Twelfth Ecumenical Council in 1215 gave sanction to rules that dealt with the following treatment of Jews: Christian princes were to keep strict watch over them lest they exact too high an interest. Baptized Jews (many baptized under force) were forbidden to retain any Jewish national customs; they were forbidden to appear in public during Easter week; they were to give tithes on their houses and property to the Church and to pay a yearly tax at the Easter festival; no Christian prince was permitted to bestow an office upon a Jew; Jews in all Christian countries were required to wear at all times a distinctive dress from the twelfth year of age distinguishing them from Christians. Thus in Germany Jews had to wear pointed hats, in Hungary a red cloth in the shape of a wheel, in England fringes of two colors, in Italy a yellow hat, in Spain males were prohibited from shaving their beards or cutting their hair under pain of a hundred lashes. That these things were never a matter of doctrine or dogma but only matters of discipline did not lessen the humiliation for the Jews of the times nor lessen the open antisemitism.

The Crusaders on their way to the Holy Land slew at least 10,000 Jews in the Rhine Valley. The Jews were expelled from Spain in 1492. The Inquisition hunted out the Marranos (Jews who were baptized but practiced their religion secretly) and between 1485 and 1498 brought to the stake some 2,000 Jews. In practice, of course, many Christians were humane enough to give the Jews help and refuge. In time even the rules of the Church changed, especially after 1532 when Clement VII ended the Inquisition. And Pope Paul of the Council of Trent gave a new spirit of justice to the Jews. Later many Catholics would come to the aid of the Jews in the Nazi madness. More than 1,800 priests were found rotting in Dachau in 1945. Pius XII eliminated the phrase the "faithless Jews" from the Catholic Good Friday service and Pope John made further changes. In fact, it was this same Pope John who made such an impression on the Jews when he met some American Jews in Rome and ran to greet them by throwing his arms around them and exclaiming, "I am Joseph your brother!" in a reference to the biblical story of Joseph and his meeting with his brothers in Egypt. The Jews have suffered much from the Christian Catholic and Shakespeare's famous speech put into the mouth of Shylock is a poignant enough reminder.

The street of prejudice between Jews and Gentiles has been a two-way one, of course, but it doesn't cancel the fact of official antisemitism in the Church. Ecumenism with the Jews can, at its least point, try to erase any traces officially left of antisemitism. At its middle point it can recognize, as with the Protestants, that there are vast differences—for the Jews the Messiah has yet to come but for the Christians He has come ("At various times . . . God spoke to our ancestors through the prophets; but in our own time, the last days, he has spoken to us through His Son." Heb 1:1). At its best, it can share the richness of our spiritual ancestor, Abraham, and rejoice in the common acknowledgement of the Fatherhood of God.

CHAPTER X

Two Unasked Questions

— 1 —

In the course of this book we have seen a basic historical principle at work: action causes reaction. So we have noticed that all of the Councils of the Church were in response to a particular crisis of the times; in the liturgy we saw that an increasingly distant ossified worship service has produced the new changes of today; that the parish is giving way to a more democratic process; that priests and sisters are reacting against a too rigid and formal life that stifled their creativity; that the youth are reacting against the materialism and postures of adults. In historical situations we saw how many of our rules and restrictions were reactions against the pressures of the times: the national parish a reaction against the strangeness of the new country; the restrictions against Protestants a reaction against their deep and long-standing discrimination against Catholics; that the legal laws of the church regarding meat on Friday, marriage and burial laws, laws against reading the Bible or attending the public schools, etc.—all were reactions against the fear of the times and were meant to defend the Catholic from the pollution of error and the stain of heresy. They were meant to protect the poor and uneducated Catholic from the false sophistication of the world in general.

We have seen how much of our own activity of renewal is a reaction against all of that! We are now grown up, educated and don't need as much paternalism and restriction and overprotection. The Reformation is over, a Catholic has been President, people are educated, knowledge has expanded and we're ready for the riches of other fine and long-standing traditions of our Catholic Church. So things are changing. Church laws are being revised.

But—but, for some, there's a terribly haunting and often publicly unasked question in this pattern of renewal; there's a disturbing anxiety as these Church laws undergo change. The problem is this: what about all those people in the past who broke those laws? Are they now in hell for eating meat on Friday, let's say, and now we can do the same thing without sin? Some people really sacrificed hard to have and raise children while today, in spite of the pope's encyclical, others are practicing birth control, and going to communion certain that in their own conscience they are doing right. Is this fair? Conversely, how about those people who *didn't* break these old laws in the past, but who kept them with great difficulty in contrast to us now who are free of so many of them and get off so much easier; again, is this fair?

To take some of the sting out of the disturbing question that people today are free of laws that bound the people of yesterday we should start off by stating simply and casually that that's life and that's the way things have always been and will be. This is not intended to sound heartless, but if you think about it, it is true. Some people have always benefited from a change of situation or change of law; others, similarly, have often been penalized. In an easy example we have the case of the first three children in a family going to the old, broken down school while the fourth child comes along and, without even realizing his good fortune, moves into the brand new school, with a theater and gym and the whole works. The other kids are mad (or pretend to be) and they cry, "It's not fair!"

"Fair" is hardly the exact word here. There's no question of justice, merely a question of progress or the change of a situation and nobody's the blame really. Or in playing Bingo, no one is more frustrated than the lady with thirteen cards hearing her neighbor with only one card cry out "Bingo." Some people must obey the alternate street parking laws in some crowded cities such as New York. Other times that rule is suspended on occasion and many thereby benefit. Some struggled to hear the crystal set, others are home enjoying color TV. The point is what was said before: that's life. States and countries have often had laws that were lifted or changed. Depending on the era in which one lived, one benefited or was restricted. Back in the 1920's prohibition forbade liquor sales and distribution. Today there's no problem but nobody is really mad who lived in the restrictive law era.

So, too, with Church laws. Her home-made laws were always capable of being changed and when they were, someone got the advantage. For instance, we are comfortable with the Friday law of abstinence being frequently called off when a Friday coincided with a holiday like Columbus Day. When that happened, a law which penalized on one Friday, liberated on another. Still, as familiar as we are with that experience, our uneasiness remains. The origin of this uneasiness is rooted in what we said in one of our previous chapters; that "we" (the teachers) never really in practice made the distinction between God's laws and the Church's laws and emotionally we tended to lump them together. Lumped together they were eternal, everlasting, immutable. This was especially true of those Church laws which we never personally encountered as having exceptions, such as some laws on marriage and the law of celibacy. But there is an even more basic cause to our uneasiness besides the failure to be taught the practical difference between God's laws and the Church's. There's the question of sin. Unlike civil laws that may alternate from age to age, there is an eternal penalty attached to some Church laws; some actually bind "under pain of sin" (we shudder to think how cavalierly this label was put on some laws of insignificance). This is an undeniable dimension, but the presence of the penalty of sin still does not essentially deny the fact that laws—even those which bind under sin—can be changed. Like those civil laws with civil penalties some people would have the advantage or disadvantage according to the era in which they lived. This bringing up of the question of sin attached to Church laws does not alter their capacity to be binding or not binding from age to age.

But, still, that uneasiness remains. "You mean that someone might be in hell for eating meat on Friday and if only he lived today, there would be no problem?" Essentially, yes; this could be the situation. Just as someone is in prison now for breaking a law that is now abrogated by the legislature. Those who violated the eighteenth amendment of Prohibition for selling liquor were jailed; today, without any such law, there is no penalty for doing that very thing. But, even here, we must be careful because when we are talking about someone being in hell for one piece of meat on Friday, we are running into a great difficulty too profound to be

treated here. We can only say that it is not true theo-
logically that a person will go to hell for one mortal sin.
God will judge our one time meat eating friend on his
whole life's moral pattern, not on one single act. Just as
the teacher gives a composite mark for a total performance so does God. He is not going to isolate one series
of laws out of the whole context of a person's religious
life. A look at the author's book *It Is The Lord!*, chapter
IV, can be of great help on this whole question.

But we must look into another side of this question.
Let's say that you or your grandparents were bound to
laws now removed; that they really struggled to keep
them and made many sacrifices. Are they any less people? Oh, it's true that some of the more inhuman laws
crushed some people. We have, unfortunately, a long
history of such cases, some quite appalling. But we're
not talking about those cases for the moment. We're just
mentioning what we probably know: a good group of
old folks, parents, friends and relatives who kept every
law of the Church and do to this day. We ask again: are
they any less people? Aren't they the fine and mature
persons whom we admire? Wasn't their sacrifice a sign
of nobility? Didn't those laws, which could have
crushed some—and did—become a challenge to them
and brought them closer to God?

After all, what essentially is the law for them but
God's will? A particular law may not indeed have been
God's will, but some neurotic legalist's will—but no
matter. God can write straight with crooked lines as the
old people say and for the genuine Catholic and the
faithful servant that's just what He did. The essence of
holiness is to do God's will. If a particular Church law
did not really reflect that will, nevertheless it was not
so opposed to it that the Spirit could not draw from its

observance an even deeper meaning and deeper substance. That's why the old folk have a faith and love
perhaps better than ours. They not only observed the
laws, but they used those laws—even the stupid and
restrictive ones—as means to find God and as *their*
means to be submissive to a Someone higher than the
written law anyway.

It is true, then, that Catholics of a former age had
more laws to obey than ourselves, but it is also true that
for many these laws, even when they hurt them to observe them, carried opportunities beyond the law's intent, opportunities to do God's will as they saw it; opportunities to move away from the law's pinch to an
expression to do something for God in the spirit of filial
sacrifice. Changing the laws for these people, then, is
really no change at all. *They* will still find meaning in
observing the Friday abstinence. At the same time the
oppression is removed for the more insightful and freedom is rightly given for the more religiously sophisticated. The changing or removing of a law does not
necessarily mean that its opportunities for holiness are
removed for that person who still wants to find something there and who voluntarily wants to persist in a
way of living that he feels can maintain his relationship
to God. There is the constant danger, as in all laws, that
law might substitute for initiative and rules might de-
generate into magic, but even these possibilites do not
cancel out the wholeness a person can bring to the most
unessential and mechanical law.

Thus some Catholic people worked well and grew
spiritually within the old framework. They saw direction even behind insensitive rules and were not particularly conscious of their deprivation or lack of freedom.
Sometimes the ultra-liberals exaggerate the horror sto-

ries and give the impression that mental and moral imprisonment was a universal phenomenon, and all Catholics were waiting to be liberated from the shackles of inhumane Church made laws. Their attempt to credit everyone else with their insights and creative drives have at times been unrealistic at its best and a most patronizing form of religious snobbery at its worst. This is not to say that some laws ought not to be changed and that due freedom must be given to us as befits sons of God. It is only to say that in the past, in the atmosphere of a paternalistic society, the cross was not as heavy for some people as it might appear in present day eyes.

— 2 —

There's the other unasked question we must come to terms with yet. It is this: does it matter to be a Catholic today? With all of the laws being changed, with us "going Protestant," with Luther's hymns in our churches and ministers at our weddings and lay boards running parishes and schools and Protestant Baptisms being accepted—what's the difference? What benefit (to put it crudely) does one get out of being a Catholic?

Even the Vatican Council II seemed to lump all Christians together. It said:

> . . All those justified by faith through Baptism are incorporated into Christ. They therefore have a right to be honored by the title of Christian and are properly regarded as brothers in the Lord by the sons of the Catholic Church.

Pope Paul himself has said:

> Are all those who have been baptized, even though separated from Catholic unity in the Church? In the true Church? In the only Church? Yes, this is one of the

great truths of the Catholic tradition and the Council repeatedly confirmed it. This doctrine is the basis for our ecumenism.

So, again, we repeat, what use to be a Catholic Christian? The answer is provided also by Vatican II. In the decree on the Constitution of the Church it says:

> The Church, constituted and organized in the world as a society, subsists in the Catholic Church, which is governed by the successor of Peter and by the bishops in union with that successor, although many elements of sanctification and of truth can be found outside of her visible structure (art. 8).

Now this is an important quotation because it tells us in theory the importance of being a Catholic. It is saying that, although holiness and truth are and can be found outside the Catholic Church, the *fullness* of these things are only in the Catholic Church and the structural and institutional fullness of Christ's kingdom are found in the Catholic Church. (In an exciting extension of this thought which we cannot develop here, that Kingdom is not the same as the Catholic Church. That all men are called to the Kingdom but not to the Church is the challenging thesis of Richard McBrien's book *Do We Need The Church?*. He sees the Church as a sign, a witness to bring the good news of the Kingdom to all men.) In an interesting footnote to the above passage from the Constitution of the Church the editors under the editorship of Walter Abbott, S.J. and Msgr. Joseph Gallagher say this:

> The Constitution here takes up the very delicate point of the relationship of the Catholic Church as it presently exists (governed by the Roman Pontiff and by the bishops in communion with him) to the Church of Christ. According to the Constitution, the Church of

> Christ survives in the world today in its institutional
> fullness in the Catholic Church, although elements of
> the Church are present in other Churches and ecclesial
> communities . . . (p. 23).

As we saw in the chapter on ecumenism, no one is
really surprised at the admission that some truth and
holiness are found in other churches. After all, they have
the living Scripture, Baptism, belief in Christ, etc. It
could not be otherwise but that these manifestations of
Christ could sanctify and nourish. But being a Catholic
means that the fullness of these realities is found in the
Catholic Church; that the completeness of the structure,
the completeness of the ways and means of holiness are
there. The pope, the bishops, the seven sacramental system, the liturgies, the priesthood—all are elements con-
stituting the full expression of Jesus' Church on earth.
To be a Catholic is to be a part of this.

There is another way of seeing oneself as a Catholic.
Visualize a staircase with four steps. On the bottom step
is the Pagan, next the Jew, next the Christian and on
top, the Catholic. Now this is an *ideal* staircase and we
mention this right off so that we will be prepared for
some actual cases. The pagan, as a human being, shares
with all the common humanity and membership in a
redeemed race. He has his lights and indeed his holiness. Yet, everything else being equal (emphatically so)
the Jew is better off. He has all of the accessibilities and
humanity of the good pagan, but in addition he has
revelation and he rejoices in the Fatherhood of God. He
has the law of Moses and a rich tradition of being chosen. Yet, everything else being equal, the Christian is
better off. He has the humanity of the pagan, the revelation of the Jew, but he also has Christ, the "first-born"
of all creation. He has the further revelation of the God

who has "made known to us his hidden purpose—such was his will and pleasure determined beforehand in Christ—to be put into effect when the time was ripe: namely, that the universe, all in heaven and on earth, might be brought into a unity in Christ" (Ephesians 1:9-10). Yet, everything else being equal, the Catholic is better off. He has the humanity of the pagan, the revelation of the Jew, the Christ-centeredness of the Christian, but he also has that fullness of which the Constitution spoke: the fullness of the church Jesus founded in his Catholic Church: the fullness of a complete sacramental life, the fullness of the priesthood, the fullness of that structure that includes the Sovereign Pontiff and the fullness of the rich traditions of East and West.

The recurring phrase "everything being equal" has been necessary because in practice no one can talk about holiness. The pagan who loves may be a better man than the Jew. The Jew who gives himself to God's service may be the saint rather than the Christian. The Lutheran who serves in Christ Jesus is closer to God than the indifferent Catholic. Obviously we cannot judge in the practical realm. Men of all persuasions can run the gamut of evil and good. It was this truism that led the jester Wamba in Scott's *Ivanhoe* to remark sarcastically, "For every Jew who is not a Christian, I can show you a Christian who's not a Christian." To be a Catholic means that the opportunities are there and the fullness should bring a more secure way to God. Whether it does and whether in the everyday practical world it *is* better to be a Catholic really depends on the individual. But in the theoretical realm, it does offer advantages.

The thing that disturbs some Catholics is the new

emphasis on the common grounds of humanity and revelation that unite all men. But this should be a cause for rejoicing. In these days of needed unity for survival it is imperative that the human race be united and stress the bonds of unity. For us Christians, it is no small thing to be able to read scripture together. The word is powerful to all who open themselves to it, be he Protestant, Jew or Catholic. We cannot confine the Spirit who will breathe where He will. Because we can share scripture or Baptism or prayer service it makes us no less a Catholic nor does it detract from the advantages of being a Catholic. In fact, it makes one more true to the title for "Catholic" means universal and the Catholic must be for all men and ready to meet all men and indeed anxious most of all to meet on the common religious grounds that mark people out not only as sons of God but as brothers of Christ.

— 3 —

It will not be remiss to give in this chapter some of the newer insights into the Church herself and her relationship to the world. We have seen that our visions of ourselves as Catholics and our particular relationship to the society around us has been shaped considerably by cultural circumstances. It is the genius of the Church to be able to stand back from time to time to redefine herself and her role in society. This, as a matter of fact, is what the Church did at Vatican II. In a newer era, in a more hospitable atmosphere the Church and her theologians are seeing a more integrated vision of the world. They are seeing not a pagan or Jewish or Christian world, but a world in itself as having been inhabited by God-become-Man. They are seeng anew an "incarnational world," a world in which, so honored and so entered into by the God-Man, nothing again can be merely secular. The whole world has become the field of God's loving activity. This world was rooted in Christ, the Word: "through him all things came to be," says St. John's Gospel. The Word and the world are inseparable. The world then is not indifferent. It is and always has been, in the design of God, Christ-related. This natural world is really not natural; it is grace-bearing. As a grace-bearing world, it speaks to us of God; it has many "ciphers" in the language of the existentialist philosopher Karl Jaspers; that is, ordinary finite events which point beyond themselves. A "cipher" can be a word, a gesture, a tear that puts man beyond himself in touch with another; what Dag Hammarskjold wrote of as "a shared, timeless happiness, conveyed by a smile, a wave of the hand." In such moments we are "lifted out of ourselves" and discover God.

When we think about it, that's the way most of us have come to know and love God. Not so much through our formal religious instruction or going to a Catholic school as from our meetings with life itself. Watching our mothers say their prayers or speak of God; seeing our fathers going off to work with regularity and fidelity, confronting sickness and even death in the family. All these living experiences pointed to something beyond and to something holy and large within the human. In a word, God is in His creation, His Christ-ed world and is revealed there. Thus "profane" things can and do convey Him: a painting done by an atheist, a story told by an agnostic, a motive that moved us—all can speak to us of God even beyond the intent of the author. If the work is truly human and truly authentic, it will carry something of God within it. Truth is Truth no matter who speaks it. There is the sacred in the secular.

There's a lot of talk these days about the secular. The

reader may be familiar with such works as *The Secular City* by Baptist theologian Harvey Cox or the works of the Jesuit Teilhard de Chardin. They are saying what we have said above: God is in an incarnational world and thus the worldly (secular) can be sacred and witness to Him. Men can look at the world not appreciating what it is but what it can be. They can see it as "becoming" something more; they can cooperate in helping creation attain its fullness (Roman 8:20-23). In this sense, any man can be and is "religious."

If this is so, then we are back to our original question, "If any man can be religious, why be especially Christians or even a Catholic Christian?" Both can be in the world, work in the world and try to bring it to its fullness. Both can work together, march together, pray together, work for better politics or government. But the difference for the Christian is that his dimensions are wider than, say, the good atheist's. Our capacity to know and to love is wider because of the conscious contact with Christ in our specifically religious lives. Michael Novak in his book *A Time To Build* put it this way:

> The Christian in Mississippi or on the subway is conscious that God lives within him, drives him on, presses upon him—not magically but by stimulating his intelligence and discriminating love until they are exercised to the utmost. Grace acts through the secular; there is no other world. But God—through the events of our lives, Scripture, the life of the Church, our conscious responses to the sacraments—illuminates our understanding of this world and enlarges our capacity to love it, so that we too, pierced by its beauty, might be willing to die for it.

> The atheist, through other events, books, communities, is pierced by the earth's beauty and dies for it without

recognizing the significance Christians give it: that it
is man's and we are Christ's and Christ is God's. . . .

Yes, the Catholic believes that Christ is at work in the
world since it is His. Whenever men act in the power of
His love, wherever there is goodness, efforts at peace,
mercy, sharing, Jesus is at work. As He himself accepted
the demands of life, lived in the world in His human
condition and gave Himself up freely to the enemy,
death, out of love for us, so at that moment He un-
leashed His Spirit into the world and that Spirit
breathes among men and among this secular world. And
His resurrection is our guarantee that as we struggle in
this world and struggle to bring the sacred from the
secular we shall not fail since He is with us.

Many of these thoughts are strange and difficult for
us. The reason is that our concept of the Church has
been so defensive for so long. Say the word "church" to
the average person or to the average adolescent, and he
thinks of that building up on the hill with its church,
school, rectory and convent. Symbolically he thinks of
his Church as a spiritual filling station, standing aloof
from the dirt of the world, a place of refuge, a bastion
of peace and a castle of mystic holiness. History has
underlined this vision. We saw that Pope Boniface said
that membership in the Church and acceptance of the
pope as sovereign were necessary for each man's salvation—even the pagan's. We saw that many of the externals of the Church were out and out borrowed from the
court: the words such as "chancery," "monsignor," "official;" the trappings such as the throne, the kissing, the
ermine; the fortress mentality.

With such a separation from the world as part of our
heritage, it is no wonder that we have difficulties with
newer emphasis. Yet emphasis is there and even Vatican

II forsook the fortress image for the image of the "Pilgrim" Church *on its way*. New insights of theology have shown us today the inadequacy of the fortress image and values like security and separateness are no longer workable in today's world. The Catholic Church, far from being apart from the world, is a part of it and exists in it. It exists in an incarnational world where there are many "authentic signs of God's presence and purpose in the happenings, needs and desires of all men of good will" (*The Church in the Modern World*, art. 11). The Church's role is thus not that of the fortress standing aside waiting for people to come into her protective walls, but rather a living and prophetic sign of Christ in the world (again, Father McBrien's book is insightful here). The Church is a community of people, not a group of buildings with headquarters at Rome; it is an assembly of witnessing Christians present in the world to help illuminate, spell out and confirm the saving reality of Jesus *wherever* the works of justice and love and mercy are being carried out.

The Catholic Church does not exist for itself. It is Servant Church, the "leaven", the "salt." The Catholic Church is that "universal" catalyst mandated to release the power of Christ in the world; it is that witnessing community to bring out the sacred from the secular; it is that "localized" and "concretized" Christ emanating into a society at large; it is the touchstone from which Christ springs to conquer the world. The Catholic Church is that many-peopled community authenticating Christ in the world. It lives, exists and works with others wherever God is made alive and wherever a "cipher" points to Him. The Church thus does not prevent others' good works but repeats her Master's words, "Do not stop him; no one who does a work of divine power in my name will be able in the same breath to speak evil of me. For he who is not against us is on our side" (Matt 9:38).

Again, what a difficult concept for many Catholics to grasp after years of emphasizing the external power and trappings of the Church! Yet, the Gospel itself bears out the image we have just described.

In a roundabout way, we have tried to answer our orignal question, "What difference does it make to be a Catholic? Why bother when we pray with the Protestants, dialogue with the Jews and make common cause with the secularists and atheists?" The answer is that, negatively, that's what we should have been doing all along only the emotionally impacted history of triumphalism and isolationism has made these natural and normal procedures seem abnormal. It is not, therefore, that we are abandoning the Church; it is that we are returning to its primary definition. Positively, to be Catholic is to be a part of this pristine tradition, it is to revel in being part of that community which is the authentic sign of Jesus in the world; it is to have genuine encounters and authentic "ciphers" in the sacraments; it is to be a part of a traditional assembly in which the pope, bishops and priests are united with us in the fullness of revelation which Jesus came to give.

It may be disappointing not to feel that as a Catholic one is a part of an elite group, an insider whose salvation is assured by the fulfilling of certain formulas and rituals; a favored son or daughter at home in all of the rooms of the house and familiar with many regulations that will guarantee one maneuvering God into granting him eternal happiness; a chosen soul distainful of the world since we "have not here a lasting city." To put aside these concepts can be disappointing and frustrating, but to put aside these concepts is also a liberation from spiritual childhood. It is to enter into life, into humanity, into the world; and not as obsessed with the fear of contamination, but filled with the witnessing power of the living Christ—to liberate Him from and to disclose Him in the secular—a power indeed gathered in many ways from one's rich Catholic heritage.

CHAPTER XI

The Liberal Catholic

– 1 –

In what may be a display of prejudice, there will be no chapter about the conservative Catholic. Presuming that the Middle Catholic tends to conservatism, then he knows his stances, his feelings and his anxieties. He doesn't always know the ins and outs of the Liberal Catholic nor does he ever appreciate the ability of the more talented liberal for self-criticism. Thus this chapter will deal with the Catholic world as the liberal sees it and the criticisms of liberals by liberals. (This will account for more than the usual number of direct quotations.)

This is not to dismiss the conservative nor to denigrate his contribution by a one or two paragraph summary but, again merely to state that our business in this book is on behalf of the mildly or wildly conservative Catholic. This conservative Catholic does just that: conserves and for that the Church must always be grateful. The conservatives have a great respect for the rich tradition of the Church. In the words of one of its most urbane and witty spokesman, William Buckley, writing in the book, *Spectrum of Catholic Attitudes,* (p. 169, 170):

> Right-wing Catholicism has to commend it a continuing acceptance of the relationship between the Church and the laity. I don't mean by this that we desire the . . . servility. . . . But do mean by it that we feel an essential faith that the Church continues to be the repository of divine mission. . . .

> . . . I do believe that the so-called Right-wing Catholics are the likelier successors to those who sweated for the survival of the word in the catacombs than are the Left-wing Catholics.

The conservative Catholic, with his respect for the Church and its traditions, is a good buffer against the excesses and fuzziness of the liberals and a genuine preserver of real values that the liberal might dismiss in a calvalier manner. The conservatives, too, of course, have their faults. They tend to over-freeze tradition and see history as one unchanging straight line rather than as a complex circle of interchanging and interacting elements. They tend to over-stress law to the exclusion of the spirit, to mistake the formula for the doctrine. The conservative tends to supress the creative thinker and sniff at progress as plot. If the liberal tends to license the conservative tends to inquisition. If the liberal flirts with fad the conservative opts for isolation.

The agony today is especially acute for the conservative as he sees his cherished traditions being demolished in the name of renewal. But, as we have seen throughout this book, many of these traditions are shallow rooted indeed. Perhaps the biggest cross for the conservative is, that in this era of liberal control of the media, he has no respected spokesman. Such spokesmen as there are for the conservative cause tend to be strident, birchite, negative, humorless and fearful. Men like Buckley, James Hitchcock and Dale Francis are exceptions, but the image of the Jeremiah conservative persists in reality. But, to the liberals, their positions and their faults.

— 2 —

Perhaps the widest catch-all phrase that conveys the liberal's major complaint can be summed up in "the institutional Church." This term covers a large area and factually and emotionally embodies the liberal rallying point. In general, for the liberal, the term "institutional Church" carries overtones of intransigence, legalism, infantilism and repression. The institutional Church is, in his eyes, the whole complex of ecclesiastical bureaucracy with all the narrow-mindedness and self-perpetuating problems of any bureaucracy. To the liberal, the institutional Church was described to a "t" in the book we mentioned earlier, *The Peter Principle*. The bureaucracy of the Church (that is, the hierarchy and chancery staffs) is filled with men who have reached their level of incompetency, but who don't even know they're incompetent. True to the Peter Principle, not only do the Super-Incompetents get retained though side tracked, but the Super-Competents are forced out of the system.

The institutional Church is suspicious of change and new ideas. It is narrow minded and cautious. It was the institutional Church that condemned Galileo who only asked that his contemporaries think of their world in a different way. Galileo's theory could upset their whole way of thinking and they were afraid to take the risk. The institutional Church is the Grand Inquisitor of Dostoevski's great novel *The Brothers Karamazov* where, in one of literature's most powerful scenes Ivan tells Alyosha the story of how Christ reappears in history, is recognized and begins to perform miracles. An aged Spanish Cardinal (The Grand Inquisitor) sees Him and arrests Him as a heretic. Christ is a threat to the established Church. No need to free men; the Church will feed them. No need for Christ to appeal to freedom and love: the law of the Church will keep the people straight. No need for Christ to lay the foundations of a kingdom of God within: the Church has a worldly kingdom, bejeweled bishops and large and costly cathedrals that will take care of the people's needs. Therefore, Christ who will upset all of this must die. To save the Church the Grand Inquisitor must burn Christ. Then Ivan ends this little parable with these words:

> . . . When the inquisitor ceased speaking he waited for some time for his Prisoner to answer him. His silence weighed down upon him. He saw that the Prisoner had listened intently all the time, looking gently in his face and evidently not wishing to reply. The old man longed for him to say something, however bitter and terrible. But He suddenly approached the old man in silence and softly kissed him. . . . That was all his answer . .

For some liberals this is the perfect picture of the institutional Church snuffing the spirit of Christ with its bureaucratic grandeur, stifling laws and meaningless legalisms. The institutional Church is the Church that turned off Luther, sided against Dreyfuss, irritated Joyce and Shaw, poked fun at Freud, laughed at Darwin, didn't bother to understand Einstein and refused to dialogue with Margaret Sanger. Father Eugene Kennedy in his book *The People Are The Church* describes it thus:

> It has been a painful embarrassment for the Church when some of its members have set themselves against

the search for a better understanding of man and his world. Most of this opposition has come from narrow minds which have clung tenaciously to rigid formulations of life. One hopes that the harrowing chapters of history which saw churchmen pitted against the advances of physical and social sciences are closed forever. Men like Galileo who looked beyond the horizons to see the world in the perspective of the universe were shamefully maltreated. So too, those like Freud who looked deeply into man were ridiculed, and their discoveries resisted until very recent times. To place oneself against truth is to sin against man the searcher and against the Holy Spirit as well (p. 108).

The all pervading legalism of the Church has stifled many spirits from the wife denied the burial of her husband in consecrated ground to the nun almost forced to stay in the convent until her dispensation came through. In the strictly spiritual realm, the legalism has multiplied sin, added laws and mechanized the sacraments into magic. The externals have become so important that Catholicism has revived Pharisaism with great success. Just gain so many indulgences and you'll add up enough credits in your column to cancel out any sin or its effects. You can come in late for Mass up to the Offertory and leave after Communion without mortal sin, although not without venial sin. You can eat up to three ounces of meat on a Friday before sin sets in. If you made the nine First Fridays you were guaranteed a seat in heaven. Confess your sins according to nature, number and circumstances; read over your list of sins and examine your conscience. Make your Easter duty and go to Mass on Sundays and Holydays. In short, the institutional Church represents a whole vast complex of rules, strictures and regulations that eventually immobilize the Christian spirit.

Like Christ in the Grand Inquisitor story, any free

spirit, any creative person threatens the establishment. If the person is really creative and really charismatic, he is usually forced out of the Church as was George Tyrrell at the beginning of the century; as almost was Cardinal Newman. Others were suspected like John Courtney Murray, Thomas Aquinas, Edward Schillebeeckx and Hans Kung. Punishment was meted out to the out and out heretic (a label determined to the satisfaction of various churchmen) and some like John Hus were put to the fire, thus giving ecclesiastical credence to the remark of Oscar Wilde, "As one read through the pages of history one is positively sickened not at the crimes of the wicked, but at the punishments of the just." Thus to the liberal the institutional Church is a Kremlin-like fortress which controls the people in every detail, crushes rebellion and suspects creativity. It is this sort of Church that has led men like Charles Davis to leave it and write *A Question of Conscience* or James Kavanagh to write *A Modern Priest Looks At His Outdated Church.*

The other areas about the institutional Church that dismay the liberal are the areas of social consciousness and morality. Here we can quote from a young Catholic liberal (24) who makes his thoughts known:

> . . . As the institutional Church adjusted itself, it became difficult for it to criticize society or demand conduct of its members which might conflict with social customs. In fact, the Church seemed unwilling to make any rigid moral requirements of its members, except for sexual ethics . . . It remained unthinkable that the American churches might, for example, condemn militarism or unfair business methods (p. 121).

> Students who went to the South, and even those who stayed home, were faced with racial hatred. This was

a kind of sin they had not heard much about. The
morality of grammar school, and even of high school,
had been personal not social. . . . Sins of omission had
been talked about, but the idea had never been applied
to social responsibility. . . .

. . . Catholic activists who were spending most of their
time arguing with other Catholics about race hatred
wondered what the point of all their theological training had been if it did not instill a vigorous moral
sensibility . . . (p. 98, 99).

This young liberal is speaking for his group. How come
the Church has been so slow in the field of moral responsibility? Hunger, poverty, racism, discrimination—
only recently has the Church in its full force and with
official weight been active here. Prior to this these matters were the concerns of small groups, but never of the
official Church. The institutional church was so preoccupied with itself and so worried about the inter-mural
rule-keeping that it forgot the weightier matters of the
law, "truth, justice and love."

Morality in general was so over-laden with rules and
strictures that the approach to God became a matter of
rule-keeping. There was no room for individual cases in
the institutional Church's morality. It was a strictly
mechanical approach. Especially in the area of sex. It
seems that sex was simply a matter of biology and marriage was a matter of sex. The woman had to render the
"debt" of intercourse under pain of mortal sin regardless
of her individual feelings, moods or desires as a person.
A marriage could be or not be dissolved depending
wholly on the mere fact of biological intercourse. The
fish-Mass-sex syndrome summarized Christian morality
and the liberal thinks that it should be more dynamic
than that.

The result of these criticisms is that the liberals are leading the fight for reform in the course of renewal. They are interested in the liturgy because the changes represent a liberation from old and meaningless forms of worship. They want the vernacular experimental Masses and a variety of worship uninstitutionalized. They are fighting the battle of freedom versus authority in the Church; they are forming their own consciences either without the Church or, as in the case of the birth control debate, in opposition to her. They want more of a voice in the running of the Church; they are insistent that they too are the Church. They want the parishes freed from the necessity of being identified with formal buildings; they want the Church restructured and, in some cases, not structured whatsoever. They are fighting for optional celibacy among the clergy as an instance of man's freedom to make his own essential choices in life. They attend the underground churches, write in favor of marriage legislation reform and want the Pope to sell the Vatican treasures and give the money to the poor.

In so many things, of course, the liberals are right. The Church should not get in the way of one being a person. They are right in seeking a more democratic way of acting, right in seeking a more personalist approach to morality, right in wanting their worship of God more meaningful.

As in all groupings, of course, there are the fringe factions who make it a practice to go to excess. Sometimes, as Father Greeley pointed out, this is a juvenile reaction against former restrictions. There are liturgies that are outrageous, wild statements against the Holy Father, rancor, insult and irreverence. The only way to deal with such is the patience and the knowledge that time will level things out. It is not these immature people we wish to criticize, but the genuine liberals about whom we can make some observations.

— 3 —

One criticism may really be not so much against the liberals as against the instant reaction to the freedom granted by Vatican II. That is, we have seen a real parade of theological fads picked up or inaugurated by Catholics. God was dead said men like Hamilton and Altizer. Or if God is alive He is talked about in the wrong way so followers of Wittgenstein will assist. Religion is encased in old non-relevant Hellenistic terms. We have Leslie Dewart to free us of this in his book *The Future of Belief.* Or religion can dialogue with the Marxists. A man named Moltmann provides a book, *The Theology of Hope.* The whole gamut of speculation is revealed and the average person is caught in a maze of applied theology and active religion. All efforts are made to evolve a "secular theology" and so create a "secular christianity". Dan Callahan, as perceptive a liberal critic as any, suggests that all these theologies are simply culture-conforming expressions. That is, the modern culture is aping religion and religion is mimicking that culture in theological terms. Callahan says:

> . . . Most of these reforms are simply culture-conforming. . . . Liturgical "renewal" reflects the culture's high valuation of intelligibility, rationality and communal participation. Collegiality is the ecclesiastical counterpart of participatory democracy. Those all-pervasive slogans, "self-fulfillment," "authenticity," and "honesty," have the sanction of an affluent society bent on consuming, releasing and enjoying. The "new" morality is an ethic made to order for a mobile people in a changing

world. The Christian sexual revolution is the product of an increasingly over-populated planet, the widespread fact of effective means of contraception, the liberation of women and the need for highly trained, well-educated technologists ("quality" rather than "quantity" people). The present emphasis in advanced theological circles on "breaking up large parishes," bringing warmth and encounter and community to religious life, correlates all too beautifully with the common sociological observation that technological man is prone to seek his identity in his private relationships rather than in the public purposes of his society (*The Critic*, June-July, 1968, pp 11-17).

Thus, theologians have been hasty and have not always perceived that their new theologies were present versions of a present culture; or, what it comes down to in practical terms, theological frivolity is a characteristic of some liberals.

A second criticism of the liberal position flows from this. In the effort to be "with" it, "it" being the process of renewal, some theologians and some reformers have cast a doubtful eye on past traditions in the Church. As we have seen, no one can doubt that some traditions were over- or under-emphasized; some were harmful and restrictive. But others were and are genuine and authentic and relevant today. One gets the impression that anything beyond forty years ago is strictly "dark ages" stuff. This would not be so bad except the impression is equally given by some liberals that *their* positions are authentic and they are the prophetic figures. They tell the more traditional Catholics that in holding on to the old time piety and legalism of their ghetto Catholicism, they are mixing up religion with culture; if one really has genuine faith inside, he doesn't need all those props to his religion.

Yet he—the reformer—very much favors *his* cultural

props and favors them as superior. He insists on his folk Masses and underground liturgies. He insists that the real Catholic must have no illusions and accept the anxieties of uncertainty and instability in life. But in doing so he is merely offering *his* solutions and patterns with which *he* has become comfortable. Becoming so tied to the culture he is in danger of becoming as obsolete as that culture. We remarked in an earlier chapter that some nuns are getting into indistinguishable everyday dress at the precise time the youth are getting into a rich variety of uniforms. Pot-smoking liturgies are as inane as secular LSD parties. Some Catholics are tossing aside the Bible for more relevant secular readings at the precise time that there is a large Fundamentalist movement on the college campuses and the kids are running to read the Bible in a most literal way. Some are inventing hyper-active liturgies at the precise moment when Oriental mysticism and meditation are becoming more appealing to a noise-polluted society. Some are throwing aside all devotions and novenas in a parish thereby creating a vacuum and not filling it with anything. In an article in *Ave Maria* James Andrews remarks:

> In our effort to be sophisticated we have gutted the parish of many of the really Christian works it had. Strangely, the seeming anachronistic works of parish societies in the past—although they too shared the fault of largely looking inward—were hardly as empty as much of what is going on in the parish today. One young priest told me that he wishes now he had found substitutes for the parish dances, Bingos, Holy Name and Legion of Mary before he gave up his active support of these works.

Thus hasty reform tied to a secular culture and overlooking the riches of the past have caused much anxiety in the Church. The liberals and reformers have something to answer for here.

As a footnote, it is interesting to notice how many of the "prophets" have realized that things have gone too far and have even repudiated some of their own initial enthusiasms. Peter Berger who wrote a book in 1961 called *The Noise of Solemn Assemblies* has now publicly repudiated much of what he said there. Justus George Lawler, editor of *Continuum*, also a liberal, has warned the theologian not to become so enamoured with literature or sociology or popular culture but "the transcendental experience. . . ." Harvey Cox, one of the high-priests of the liberal movement who wrote the very popular *The Secular City* has also denied much of what he wrote there. Martin Marty, the Lutheran theologian and frequent contributor to Catholic magazines, has warned the Catholic Church over a too hasty neglect of her own rich traditions. Andrew Greeley writes frequently warning of excess and bringing his common sense attitudes to those who want to do away with all church structures or who are so delighted at retreat times with such fads as sensitivity sessions. Dan Callahan has been brave enough to criticize the liturgy and the document of Vatican II on that subject.

Recently it has been brought to light that the famed Trappist, Thomas Merton, so solidly identified with the liberal cause had critical things to say about renewal. In the February 11, 1970, book supplement to the *National Catholic Reporter,* James F. Andrews reports on Merton's unpublished opinions, as expressed by the monks who knew him well:

> "Father Louis (Merton) thought that renewal had gotten out of whack, that it has become another mass movement, another form of the same old conformity. That

cultural criteria are being used and that as a result all studies and explorations conform to the expected progressive stand. Louis' whole history made him a nonconformist although he was not a rebel", Eudes says.

Abbot Flavian backs up Eudes' observations. "Louis was with the people in the modern church who wanted radical change. But he was never on a bandwagon. He saw a lack of depth in what was being said and done. Thus, again his role of critic would have pushed him into action. He felt that we should get rid of things that get in the way of what we're trying to do. But that did not mean getting rid of what we're trying to do. He thought the movement was getting too superficial."

Andrews quotes from Merton's unpublished talks criticizing the lack of prayer as rationalized by some priests, the sisters in the ghettos, married priests and the tendency to locate God only in the "horizontal" and no longer in the transcendental. Again, all these men, from Lawler to Merton are respected names in the liberal camp.

Another criticism of the liberals is their tendency to overstate cases. They look back, for example, and see themselves as the early Christians, a kind of free-floating group that believed without formulated dogmas, were faithful without rules and were willing to die in utter sincerity for their cause. But, on the contrary, it was the "pagan" Romans who were tolerant in their day and quite enlightened as to minority groups. As a matter of fact those early Christians were responsible for a real onslaught against the Synagogue and planted the seeds of Christian antisemitism. And when Christianity eventually supplanted the Roman Empire it practiced a repressiveness towards belief far more severe and took on all the court and medieval trappings of society. If this was the evolution of those early Christians, some wonder about the analogy to the reformers of today. They also overstate their happy desire for a "structure-less" community. Again, Father Greeley comes off with a telling comment on this sort of thing in *The Hesitant Pilgrim*:

> . . . The idea of a pneumatic Church is an attractive one and always has been. A handful of dedicated Christians working in a community in almost invisible fashion, exuding good will and love, and unconcerned about mundane things such as finance, administration, and communication, sounds terribly appealing. But even if it were possible for a community of humans to exist without a formal structure (and it is quite impossible), those who would object to a structured Church and would prefer a pneumatic one should take the matter up with the Founder who wanted His Church to be a thoroughly human organization and seemed prepared to accept the fact that in this human organization there would be all kinds of human imperfections.

> . . . The trouble with angry, alienated revolutionaries is that they can't win; they really don't want to win. They are what Irving Howe calls the *kamakazie* radicals who desire to pull down and destroy so that a fresh new start can be made. But they ignore the lessons of history that real growth is always organic, and that true progress usually comes from reforms of existing structures rather than from the creation of brand new ones pp. xiv, xv).

"Structure" and "Community" go together no matter how loosely. To be a member of society is to be in some way structured. As we also saw in an earlier chapter, the liberals overstate the suffering and oppression by the Church to her members. Not everyone was crushed by oppressive laws and inhumane legalisms. There was too much of this, as we have admitted, but there was not the world-wide enslavement of a groaning and beaten people as some would have us believe. At least many grandparents and parents do not give that impression. James Hitchcock, the only conservative quoted at length in this chapter, states the case well in the Jesuit magazine *America:*

> The greatest achievement of the traditional Church was to articulate meaning and coherence in the lives of millions of people whose existence would otherwise have been bleak and hopeless. It is a purpose that the Church still serves for innumerable people of all social classes, although the severe decline of the Church's public prestige has no doubt weakened this function considerably . . . The Catholic radical is embarrassed by this fact to a degree, since it does not fit his contention that the Church is a total failure, but he can easily dispose of the phenomenon by reaching for another of the social sciences—psychology. The meaning that very many people have apparent'y found in religion is a form of neurosis: it is a search for security, a fleeing from life, in that sense a negation of the gospel.

> Since no one really knows the interior spiritual life of the millions who remain adherents of the Church, such comments are at best hasty and at worst cruel and arbitrary, reflecting in the radical an intellectual colonialism that under other circumstances wou!d horrify him. Does the remark that the Church is a 'heaven'y insurance policy' really express accurately the faith of the businessman, or is it a crude attempt to fit theology to the American idiom? Is it not likely that among those many who still finger their beads and light candles there is much genuine longing for God and desire to do His will? *(America,* September 13, 1969, p. 157)

Again, the Church may be chided for the lack of social consciousness and there remains the scandal of our social indifference to the poor and needy. Still, this is not to say that *nothing* was done. Those schools and orphanages and hospitals did not materialize out of nowhere. Besides, it is not altogether to be wondered at that American Catholics did not do more in the way of social activity. We have seen something of our early history; we were an immigrant minority, struggling not only for a living but for tolerance in Protestant America. We had a great deal of internal problems. No one blames the Negro of today for not carrying the banner high for the American Indian. We recognize that the Negro has his own battle to fight and his own freedom to achieve. This situation is not dissimilar to the American Catholic in the early days spent in America.

Finally, there seems to be a touch of Pelagianism in some liberals. Pelagianism is an early heresy which held that man could gain grace and get to heaven by his own unaided merits. Some liberals have an enormous faith in man to perfect himself without assistance. They tend to put a great burden on man's conscience in the guise of the freedom of the sons of God. They give the impression that man, if let free, will himself always choose the right, form a right conscience and act altruistically. Commandments and sin are out; freedom and the promptings of the Holy Spirit are in. For many people, however, there is a desire and a need for one freedom that the liberals often overlook, the freedom to be restrained. This is no contradiction, but rather the freely accepted self-knowledge that one is prone to sin and weakness (call it original sin or psychological complexes or what have you), and that therefore one welcomes the inhibitions imposed by law to be oneself. It would be ideal that one should be truly human and Christian solely from one's inner resources, but, alas, this is not so. Most people look to outside guidelines and laws to help them to be what they cannot be alone.

— 4 —

On balance, we owe much to the liberals. If they have their faults, they also have what the conservatives often lack: insight, vision and a touch of poetry. Too often the Church has been a Church of the conservatives and has had no room for the freer spirits of the liberals. Too often the Church has, as we have seen, met the liberals with suspicion and hostility. Too often the Church has stifled the creativity of the liberal mind only, as so often it has happened, to accept that creativity in another day and age. In a sense Christ was a liberal, trying to free men from the excessive and restrictive Pharisaism of the time, preaching tolerance, the love of God—love of man interconnection, preaching an interior morality and freedom of the Spirit. He was put to death by His Grand Inquisitors. Paul had to defend himself at the first Council at Jerusalem against the conservatives who really wanted a Jewish Christianity. Paul's success changed the whole course of Christianity. The ultra-conservative Church suspected, hunted out, put to the stake, condemned the liberals of the ages. The liberals have to their credit the constant spirit of renewal within the Church, adaptability and progress. They have always been our prophets. It is not always easy to tell the authentic ones (the inauthentic ones being capable of much harm), but whoever they are, we must listen to their voices.

CHAPTER XII

Underneath

— 1 —

Seldom does the Middle Catholic realize that much of his distress about renewal has its genesis from another source; that the true causes lie buried underneath and indeed may have nothing to do with renewal itself. In other words, it isn't that he is always upset about what's going on in his Church: it's that, prior to and concomitant with renewal in religion, he is being torn apart by renewal from without. It would not be so bad if there were only change in the Church *or* only change without—but changes in *both* areas are too much to take. When the Middle Catholic rails against the newest bit of renewal, often he is ventilating unconsciously his deeply threatened state over the whole deteriorating society in which he lives. All of his old values are being dismembered and his Church (he feels) ought not to be a part of that dismemberment. Rather, it ought to be the Physician which heals the riffs in his heart.

This point is crucial. The style of our society where change is almost the hallmark is very hard on the human organism. And if realistically titled books like Toffler's *Future Shock*, Rosenfeld's *The Second Genesis* or Taylor's *The Doomsday Book* are in any way accurate then many older Middle Folk (Catholic or not) may well be glad that they are near the end of their lives. Life is just too fast these days; old, cherished values are just too turned over; the velocity of history is just too swift. Arthur Schlesinger, Jr., catches the tempo when he writes:

> This increase in the velocity of history dominates all aspects of contemporary life. First of all, it is responsible for the unprecedented unstability of the world in which we live. Science and technology make, dissolve, rebuild and enlarge our environment every week; and the world alters more in a decade than it used to alter in centuries. This has meant the disappearance of familiar landmarks and guideposts that stabilized life for earlier generations. It has meant that children, knowing how different their own lives will be, can no longer look to parents as models and authorities. Change is always scary; uncharted, uncontrolled change can be deeply demoralizing. It is no wonder that we moderns feel forever disoriented and off balance; unsure of our ideas and institutions; unsure of our relations to others, to society and to history; unsure of our own purpose and identity.

> . . . Indeed, no social emotion is more widespread today than the conviction of personal powerlessness, the sense of being beset, beleaguered and persecuted . . . .

> If the crisis seems today more acute in the United States than anywhere else, it is not because of the character of our economic system; it is because the revolution wrought by science and technology have gone further here than anywhere else. As the nation at the extreme frontier of technological development, America has been the first to experience the unremitting shock and disruptive intensity of accelerated change . . . . (NEWSWEEK, July 6, 1970)

For the Middle Catholic experiencing the truth of these words there is, perhaps, a more than usual longing

for peace, meaning and interpretation which traditionally he might expect from his Church. But, when the
Church itself seems to be shaken, unsure and change-
able then the sense of betrayal which we spoke of in
another chapter becomes acute. The Church built upon
the rock now seems to be floundering upon sand. The
Catholic who looked to the Church as a fortress of protection in a time of change discovers a Church changing
with the world. Once more, then, the point is that many
Middle Catholics' especial distress over Church renewal
is considerably heightened by the pressures of persistent change in their *daily* lives. There are, however,
other elements of cultural change which make Church
change more unpalatable.

For one thing, there's a minority activist group in the
land, mostly students and some adults, who threaten to
turn the Middle American's (and the Catholic's) world
upside down. Most Middle Catholics reflect their coun-
terparts' values of hard work and success. They too have
worked hard, pulled themselves up in the world by their
boot straps and have sacrificed much. They gave up
much to send their children to school. Perhaps the educated among them worked their way through college.
It is no wonder that if the activist student, say, rejects
hard work and discipline the Middle American feels
that the rules of the game are being unjustly changed.
If *he* had to work for what he got, why should others
distain it or not feel the same compulsion to work? Why
should militant students or "undeserving" blacks simply
waltz in to enjoy what they, the Middle Americans,
worked so hard for? Why should they who have not
worked be equal to those who have? That black students should be let into college without an entrance
test or requirements while they had to study and sweat

for the same thing seems grossly unfair. That families should seemingly receive welfare from their tax money while they had to sweat for the good things of life seems terribly unjust. That the young should have and want sexual freedom while they believe in strict marital fidelity seems a privilege which they, the young, have not earned and which was denied to those of the Protestant ethic. As Lane and Lerner explain:

> Campus violence destroys the Middle-American image of education as granted to the most judicious, self-disciplined and deserving; the narrow perspectives of some radicals destroy the Middle-American belief that education creates solicitude for the working class and breath of perspective; the radical championing of the poor undermines the Middle-American conviction that the poor and the blacks deserve their poverty. All this undermines the Middle-American sense of the justness of American society.
>
> . . . The counterculture sex and drug mores, with their call for greater relaxation and acceptance of instinctual drives, threaten the morality and emotional styles of the Middle-American in even more apparent ways and contribute to his sense that his inner as well as his outer worlds are falling apart. (*Psychology Today*, November, 1970)

Indeed the flux of his inner and outer world is what makes the Middle Catholic's stress so acute today; and when the Church itself seems to be taken in by the world and itself champions the causes of poverty, race equality and equal opportunity or gives in to James Forman's demands for money for the black community in "reparation," then the frustration of betrayal knows no bounds. Whether all this church activity is right or wrong is not the issue here. The issue, once more, is that the Middle Catholic brings pre-conditioned anxiety about his life style and the hurts of an "unjust" society to his church. Expecting to find quiet, peace, solitude, stability and a hierarchy of established values he finds instead another variation of the problems he was seeking to escape.

There's another result of multi-leveled change. It is this: the Middle Catholic is not only becoming unsure about himself and his values but whatever values are left seem to be built on dwindling plausibility as his church (he believes) waters down doctrine and practice; and if the credibility of what he believes is called into question then the disaster is total. As Peter Berger has so well pointed out in his excellent book *A Rumor of Angels*, we are social beings and our sociability includes what we think, believe and know (even mistakenly) about the world. Since most of what we feel we know is taken on the authority of others then only if these others continue to back up and confirm our body of knowledge does it remain plausible. It is precisely just such shared knowledge and values that give us confidence as we move through life. The moment when, for some reason, *our* knowledge and our value system is no longer shared with others and supported by others then we become anxious. Our knowledge now becomes a defensive one: believing in the face of tolerant disbelief; holding on to those values which for many now no longer have any meaning. All of a sudden we may find ourselves upset in our own minds, unsafe, insecure. Mr. Berger goes on to explain:

> For example, the maintenance of the Catholic faith in the consciousness of the individual requires that he maintain his relationship to the plausibility structure of Catholicism. This is, above all, a community of Catholics in his social milieu who continually support

this faith. It will be useful if those who are of the greatest emotional significance to the individual (the ones whom George Herbert Mead called significant others) belong to this supportive community—it does not matter much if, say, the individual's dentist is a non-Catholic, but his wife and his closest personal friends had better be. Within this supportive community there will then be an ongoing conversation that, explicitly and implicitly, keeps a Catholic world going. Explicitly, there is affirmation, confirmation, reiteration of Catholic notions about reality. But there is also an implicit Catholicism in such a community. After all, in everyday life it is just as important that some things can silently be taken for granted as that some things are reaffirmed in so many words. Indeed, the most fundamental assumptions about the world are commonly affirmed by implication—they are so "obvious" that there is no need to put them into words. Our individual, then, operates within what may be called a specifically Catholic conversational apparatus, which, in innumerable ways, each day confirms the Catholic world that he coinhabits with his significant others. If all these social mechanisms function properly, his Catholicism will be as "natural" to him as the color of his hair or his belief in the law of gravity. He will, indeed, be the happy possessor of an *anima naturaliter christiana,* a "naturally Christian soul."

Such flawlessness in the plausibility structure is unlikely. For this reason, the supportive community (in this instance, the institutional church) provides specific practices, rituals, and legitimations that maintain the faith over and beyond its basic maintenance by a Catholic social milieu. This, of course, includes the whole body of pious practices, from the formal sacraments to the private reassurance rites (such as prayer) recommended to the individual. It also includes the body of knowledge (in the Catholic case, vast in volume and of immense sophistication) that provides explanation and justification for each detail of religious life and belief. And in this instance, of course, there is a staff of highly trained experts as well, who mediate the therapeutic and legitimating machinery to the individual. The details of all of this vary in different circumstances, especially as between a situation in which the plausibility structure is more or less coextensive with the individual's over-all social experience (that is, where Catholics constitute the majority) and a situation in which the plausibility structure exists as a deviant enclave within the individual's larger society (that is, where Catholics are a cognitive minority). But the essential point is that the plausibility of Catholicism hinges upon the availability of these social processes.

. . . It is relatively easy, sociologically speaking, to be a Catholic in a social situation where one can readily limit one's significant others to fellow Catholics, where indeed one has little choice in the matter, and where all the major institutional forces are geared to support and confirm a Catholic world. The story is quite different in a situation where one is compelled to rub shoulders day by day with every conceivable variety of "those others", is bombarded with communications that deny or ignore one's Catholic ideas, and where one has a terrible time even finding some quiet Catholic corners to withdraw into.

Now here we have a further elaboration about the causes of the Middle Catholic anxiety. If teachers and members of our own Church are not apparently holding to traditional teachings, where does that leave the Middle Catholic but on ground considerably underminded? The credibility of his whole religious beliefs are being eroded! The plausibility of his whole life's fabric is suddenly being called into doubt. It may be all right for some teachers and theologians to speculate about several First Parents or about sinless premarital sex; it may be all right for the Church to call off the Lenten fast and the Friday abstinence; it may be all right for the

Another approach we have used is the reminder that we, the teachers, have compounded the present emotional problem to renewal by failing to make proper distinctions in the past; that we tended to lump together the deposit of faith with mere custom or cultural extensions; that we equated in practice God's law with ecclesiastical law; that we over-protected our "little ones" and donned the paternal role so effectively that what "Father says" or what "Sister says" became more powerful than the Ten Commandments; that we set up an elaborate system of rules and regulations and had so many ready-made answers that the average Catholic had complete trust in his Church in exact proportion as he distrusted himself in religious matters. When, as we have seen, we are now beginning to make the proper distinctions and are, in effect, pushing the people more out on their own they are unstable, uneasy and bewildered. To answer with "what do *you* think?" to one conditioned to come for answers can be almost traumatic. As Father Joseph Gallagher put it, "We've drugged the people for so long and now we've taken away their drugs."

But, there have been mistakes also as we have shown: Dan Callahan remarking that many Church changes are imitations of cultural changes; teachers tearing down old traditions without replacing new ones or even giving the old ones their validity; a busyness in the liturgy and a busyness in the social field with a resulting over-involvement of the Church at the expense of the spirit, silence and contemplation. And now we can add more criticisms here. For example, William Braden in his book *The Age of Aquarius* notes how the liberal churchmen are still looking for the pews to fill up with concerned young people for whose benefit one supposes many changes were made and who supposedly complained that the Church was too "other worldly" to really be meaningful to this world. He quotes a young medical student who became a Buddhist, leaving his Protestant faith saying, "I quit when my church became relevant." Braden gives a telling quote from socialist Michael Harrington who wrote, "The Church must fight for the earthly implication of the heavenly values it affirms; it can never again divorce God from the Negroes, the poor, those dying in war, and the rest of humanity. But over and above that witness to the temporal meetings of the eternal there must be the assertion of the eternal itself." In other words there does seem to be lost in the efforts of renewal the question which asks whether the real mission of the Church is not so much to be active itself as to sustain people in their personal and social encounters with the world; to offer them a supra-worldly source of strength that could heal them as well as inspire them.

There may be the danger too that too quick changes without accompanying education, the introduction of better values and the reaffirmation of the old values might produce a valueless generation. Some people temperamentally need more guidance than others. All need a deepening of their spiritual values. Where this is being done the liberated Catholic grows and becomes truly a free "son of God." Where this is not done, then alienation is just around the corner. Father Eugene Kennedy in his book *A Time For Love* quotes a Harvard sophomore who complains about the upbringing of his own life. He says:

If I had been brought up in Nazi Germany—supposing I wasn't Jewish—I think I would have had an absolute set of values, that is to say, Nazism, to believe in. In modern American society, particularly in the upper-middle class, a very liberal group, where I am given no religious background, where my parents always said to me, "if you want to go to Sunday School, you *can*," or "if you want to take music lessons, you *can*," but "it's up to *you*," where they never did force any arbitrary system of values on me—what I find is that with so much freedom, I am left with *no* value system, and in certain ways I wish I had a value system forced on me, so that I could have something to believe in. (Steven Kelman, "These Are Three of the Alienated," *The New York Times Magazine,* Oct. 22, 1967, p. 39)

Lack of continuing education for the people can foster the same kind of betrayal in the Church. Change alone without growth can lead to religious-value alienation. Add to this the irony that where before in the Church there was no room for the truly charismatic figure (the "Super-Competent"), *now* there seems to be no room for anyone else. Everyone is a prophet. Everyone must "do his own thing." "Our" thing, built on shared values, has still yet to be investigated.

There are two more points we must briefly make before we close this chapter. One is that there are already good signs that a reaction to an over-activism in the Church is settling down. Seminaries, for example, are reporting that the seminarians themselves are making a return to the old and tried formulas of meditation, morning Mass and prayer. The Pentecostal movement at least represents an interest in the Spirit. Father Greeley in his book *The Friendship Game* notes the swing back to silence and meditation; that Zen is quite popular, campus meditation is "in" and mysticism is very much alive. Even hyper-active young people, he tells us, have opted for the "old-fashioned" retreat where there were periods of solitude and silence.

The other point is the predictable reaction to all change by counter groups within the Church. Groups like CUF (Catholics United for the Faith), etc., are seeking to lobby to bring back some of the old ways and to prevent the erosion of "true" religion. They are fighting for religious integrity but they, unknowingly, are also fighting for plausibility. As we pointed out in the first part of this chapter man needs moral support if his beliefs are to survive. That's why we said organizations like CUF were quite predictable. Disturbed and frightened people will tend to group to preserve their basic life's values if they feel such values are being threatened and perhaps threatened into extinction. In any case such groups may be valuable in at least posing questions and forcing those engaged in renewal to take second and long range looks at what they are doing.

Renewal is a contextual thing. It really ought not to be considered apart from the times we live in. Our social equilibrium is off balance and this makes change in the Church more difficult to deal with, more emotionally difficult to assimilate. The Middle Catholic should try to stand back, as it were, from the whirl of renewal and see it more objectively, acknowledging the anxious state he brings to it yet reaffirming once more Paul's proclamation and guarantee "Jesus Christ, the same yesterday, today and forever."

CHAPTER XIII

Renewal and the Middle Catholic

— 1 —

This chapter will be brief—an epilogue, as it were, on the subject of renewal and the Middle Catholic. As we mentioned in the introduction to this book we were not going to deal at all with the "ultra" Catholic on either side of the renewal question. Dialogue is often difficult with them, mostly because they are so defensive. They are threatened. The ultra conservative Catholic shows his defensiveness by closing his eyes and ears to anything that is new. He tends to retreat to his old time religion and neither his parish priest nor the pope himself is going to change his mind. This is the Catholic who probably hasn't grown over the years, hasn't matured in his emotional or religious life. By working himself into one religious routine, by becoming so comfortable with one set way, he has closed himself off from further growth. Anything which might disturb his religious castle is turned off. Deep down he lacks self confidence. Deep down he must defend his old time religion, even some of its absurd aspects, because once he admits the possibility and desirability of renewal, he must rearrange his whole life. He must expose himself to the pain of growth. He must run the risk of emptying certain cherished notions without the assurance that anything more satisfying will replace them. Because he is afraid to take the risk, he becomes hardened in his ways, defensive and angry. He won't even study or look at the other side. He will grab on a few frivolities and outright stupidities of renewal and extend them to include everything whatever. "If that is renewal, it's not for me!" he can exclaim triumphantly. The ultra conservative is basically afraid.

But so too is the ultra liberal. He is afraid from a different point of view. He is afraid of introspection, of patiently building religious stability. He may even lack a certain amount of self discipline and so becomes something of a theological gadfly. In his view, everything must come down, everything in the past was wrong, every Catholic was a religious barbarian, every Pope was political, every bishop closed minded, every institution bureaucratic. He doesn't alight long enough to think, assess, synthesize. He too is afraid: afraid of his thoughts, afraid of systematic work, afraid of genuine dialogue. In some cases, it is hard to tell how much religious frantic concern is genuine and how much is symptomatic of problems in other areas of his life. If the ultra conservative is threatened by the outside invading his inside stability, the ultra liberal is afraid of the inside invading his outside activism.

Between these two extremes lay many of the genuine scholars and patient men on both sides. Men with ideas, with interest, with a willingness to dialogue, a willingness to pose and listen to new ideas. Men willing to work, to research, to pray, to think quietly. Men willing sometimes to be bold in their expression and thoughts but always with the understood humility that they may be wrong.

Between these two extremes lay also the Middle Catholics. People afraid, yet open; fearful yet patient. They are people who are perplexed but who do want answers. It isn't that they disagree with everything about renewal. Probably for the average Middle Catholic it's almost entirely a question of education. He wants to know why and what. Emotionally he may understandably be quite attached to some old ways, but he is willing to learn what is behind the new. The new will hardly get his emotional allegiance like the old, but he will give it his intellectual assent if he understands it. It is hoped that this book has aided in that understanding.

What now is left? Perhaps just two more points: one, a suggested program for the Middle Catholic; the other, final words of encouragement. The suggested program is a four-step procedure on what practical steps the Middle Catholic can take to maintain his balance in this era of renewal.

First of all, the Middle Catholic should self educate himself. As we have seen all throughout this book, there are many points of information that were perhaps new and surprising. That one has read this book at all is a step forward; but reading this book also indicates how much more the education process must continue. A beginning to further education would be to continue one's reading. Some excellent and informative books are listed in the bibliography which appears in the appendix following. In addition, the Middle Catholic should keep alert to the magazines and newspapers. *St. Anthony Messenger, U.S. Catholic and Jubilee, Liguorian, The Sign, America* are all interesting magazines that can keep one up to date. Newspapers such as *Our Sunday Visitor, Twin Circle* are helpful.

We would like to mention *Triumph* magazine and the newspaper *The National Catholic Reporter*. Both are extremes, both tend to hold up one valid point out of context for real living and real renewal, but they are interesting. Next, he should get into some study groups either in his parish or in another. He should attend lecture courses and adult courses when they are offered.

Secondly, he should get involved in his parish if he can afford the time. There probably will be some parish council activities in his parish in the near future. Or he should stay in his societies. If such societies are in danger of becoming extinct, he should ask himself why. What can he do either to revitalize them or re-route them? The same with parish devotions. If the Novena has dropped off to a trickle, he should see if enough people are interested to revive it. Or else, see if devotions with new slants might be profitable.

Thirdly, the Middle Catholic should be active in liturgical participation. Just to sit in the pew and stew is not the answer. For the sake of his own satisfaction, he should get involved. He should go to a parish, if his own is not liturgically up-to-date, and take part in the offertory procession. He should stand around the altar, drink from the chalice, etc. where these things are permitted. Then he should see if he really minds these things. Then he should see if he really felt something new in his participation, a further dimension of what the Mass can mean.

Finally, he should continue to deepen his own spiritual life. New or old, one's knowledge and love of God are still primary. Renewed or reactionist this is still the goal. He should pray and pray to the Holy Spirit that He guide His Church during these times. He should continue his faithfulness to Mass and the sacraments, his prayer life. He should be a witness to those leading the church renewals and reforms. Let them see that whatever the faults of the old way, it did possess, by the grace of God, the power to make one a good Catholic.

— 2 —

With the above listed as a practical program of action, let us conclude with some words of encouragement to the Middle Catholic.

1. The Middle Catholic, in the midst of current renewal, should not lose his pride. Fidelity and good works have characterized him throughout the past decades. If he is not quite sure about the present changes, not quite comfortable this is understandable. So many things represent such a radical departure from the old ways. But he should keep his pride because of the good things he has, by the grace of God, wrought. The endless charities, the thousands of splendid evidences of his charity and concern dotted throughout the land should make him realize what has been accomplished. The countless acts of faith, the devotions, the genuine acts of religion should make him aware of how truly and effectively Holy Mother Church has nourished millions of Catholics in any age. The Middle Catholic should be proud.

2. The Middle Catholic should be critical. Some of renewal is fad, some of renewal, as we have seen in this book, is not above a second look and in need of reassessment. The only requirement for the Middle Catholic, if he is to be an honest and knowledgeable critic, is to increase his learning and to promote his self education, so that he knows whereof he speaks. This book has tried

to help in this way also. It has tried to give not only information, but information in perspective.

3. The Middle Catholic should be brave. This may sound condescending, but it is not meant to be. After all, we *are* in a brand new world and the scripts and blueprints of the past are of little use. Every day brings new and sometimes frightening possibilities. Man does seem to be out to either destroy himself or pollute himself off the planet. Men seemed to have lost perspective and greed and lust for money have again exploited man only this time to a dangerous and threatening degree. Beauty, civility and humanity seem to be disappearing from the scene. There are poets like Archibald MacLeish who are raising their voices against uninterrupted technology; they are asking men to ask themselves whether all progress is really an event of *human* progress or whether progress means winding up with a planet full of deodorant cans, macadam and machines—but no people. There is a certain madness to think that what *can* be done, *should* be done. But, again, the Middle Catholic should be brave because he has his faith, his God and the promises of Christ. One benefit of the old time religion is that it did give him that.

4. The Middle Catholic should be forgiving. He should be forgiving not only in the sense that he realizes that in the past he may have received a false emphasis but forgiving in that he does not sulk at what benefit authentic renewal has given to latter day Catholics. Rather, he rejoices. He realizes that those who came at the last hour can receive the same wage as those who, like themselves, have borne the heat of the day. God, after all, is Master of His gifts. Else the Middle Catholic might find himself part of that scene so well described by Louis Evely in his book, *That Man Is You:*

little to cheer about. But life is a celebration and Christ is our Joy and the Resurrection is our pledge of life everlasting. Renewal is not a threat, after all, nor is it, as we have amply seen in this book, new on the religious scene. In fact, the persistency and constancy of renewal in the pages of history should make one realize that the Spirit of God is very much at work; it should make one realize that the Church is divinely inspired, for such genius at constant self-renewal is a sign of God at work.

The Church we know is the Church of today. No use looking back. It's the future that is here. To retreat to the false nostalgia of the "good old days" is to deny one's apostleship. Christ is here in the 1970's. Each Middle Catholic must do his best to interpret Him to his own era, his own times. Renewal need not mean loss; it may mean gain. The Middle Catholic has his choice.

Changes in the Mass

(The following is the text of a talk given on November 19, 1969, by Pope Paul VI.)

We wish to draw your attention to the event which is about to take place in the Latin Catholic Church and which will have its obligatory application in the Italian dioceses starting from the first Sunday of Advent, which this year falls on November 30. That is, the introduction in the liturgy of the new rite of the Mass. Mass will be celebrated in a form considerably different from the one we have been accustomed to celebrate for the past four centuries, since the time of St. Pius V after the Council of Trent.

There is something surprising, extraordinary about the change, since the Mass is considered the traditional and intangible expression of our religion, of the authenticity of our faith. We may ask ourselves: Why such a change? And of what does this change consist? What are the consequences implied for those who will attend Holy Mass?

The replies to these questions and to other similar ones provoked by such a singular innovation will be given to you fully and will be extensively repeated in all the churches, in all the publications of a religious nature and in all the schools where Christian doctrine is taught. We exhort you to pay attention to them, thus endeavoring to clarify and to deepen somewhat the stupendous and mysterious notion of the Mass.

But meanwhile, through this brief and elementary discourse, let us try to remove from your minds the first and spontaneous difficulties raised by this change in relation to the three questions it immediately brought to our minds.

Why such a change? Our reply: It is attributable to a will expressed by the recently celebrated ecumenical council.

The council says: "The rite of the Mass is to be revised in such a way that the intrinsic nature and purpose of its several parts, as also the connection between them, can be more clearly manifested, and that devout and active participation by the faithful can be more easily accomplished.

"For this purpose the rites are to be simplified, while due care is taken to preserve their substance. Elements which, with the passage of time, came to be duplicated or were added with but little advantage, are now to be discarded. Where opportunity or necessity demands, other elements which have suffered injury through accidents of history are now to be restored to the earlier norm of the Holy Fathers" (Constitution on the Sacred Liturgy, no. 50).

Therefore, the reform which is about to be divulged corresponds to an authoritative mandate of the Church. It is an act of obedience, it is a fact of the Church's consistency with itself, it is a step forward in its authentic tradition, it is a demonstration of faith and vitality to which we must all promptly adhere.

It is not an arbitrary decision. It is not a fleeting or optional experiment. It is not the improvisation of some amateur. It is a law framed by authoritative scholars of sacred liturgy, discussed and studied at length. We would do well to welcome it with joyous interest and to apply it with punctual and unanimous observance.

This reform puts an end to the uncertainties, to the discussions, to harmful arbitrary abuses and calls us to that uniformity of rites and sentiments which is proper to the Catholic Church, the heir and prolonger of that first Christian community which was wholly "one heart and one soul" (Acts 4:32).

Choral prayer in the Church is one of the signs and one of the strengths of its unity and of its catholicity. The change which is about to take place cannot break or disturb this chorality, but must confirm it and make it resound with a new spirit, a breath of youth.

Another question: Of what does the change consist? You will see it. It consists of many new ritual prescriptions which will demand, in the beginning particularly, some attention and some care. Personal devotion and the sense of community will make the observance of these new prescriptions easy and pleasant.

But let it be very clear: nothing has changed in the substance of our traditional Mass. Some may perhaps allow themselves to be unfavorably impressed by some particular ceremony or by some suppressed rubric, as if this were an alteration, or hid an alteration, or were a lessening of the truths of Catholic faith, acquired forever and authoritatively sanctioned, almost as if the equation between the law of prayer and the law of belief were thereby compromised.

But this is not true in any way. First of all, because the rite and pertinent rubrics are not in themselves a dogmatic definition and may be rendered by a theological qualification of a different value according to the liturgical context to which they refer. They are gestures and terms referred to a religious action lived and living; of an ineffable mystery of divine presence, not always realized in a univocal form, an action which theological critics alone can analyze and express in logical formulae that are satisfying.

Then, the Mass of the new order is and remains, if anything, with greater evidence as regards some of its aspects, the same Mass. The unity between the Supper of Christ, in which the Lord, by making the bread and wine into His Body and His Blood, instituted the sacrifice of the New Testament. He wished that by virtue of His priesthood, conferred on the apostles, it be renewed in its identity but offered in a different way, that is in an unbloody and sacramental way, in perennial memory of Him until His final return (cf. De La Taille, Mysterium Fidei, elucid. IX).

If in the new rite you find that greater clarity is shown to indicate the relationship between the liturgy of the word and the properly Eucharistic liturgy (as if this one answer were to realize the other), or if you observe how the assistance of the faithful is demanded at the celebration of the Eucharistic sacrifice—the faithful who are the Mass and fully feel the (sense of) the Church. Or yet if you see illustrated other wonderful properties of our Mass, do not believe that this is an attempt to alter the genuine and traditional essence. But rather, appreciate how the Church wishes to give greater efficacy through this new and diffused language to its liturgical message. Observe also the attempt to bring the Mass closer to each of its sons and to the entire people of God in a more and direct pastoral way.

And thus we answer the third question we have set for ourselves: What are the consequences going to be of the innovations of which we are speaking? The foreseen, or rather, the desired consequences are those of a more intelligent, more practical, more enjoyable, more sanctifying participation of the faithful in the liturgical mystery. That is to say, of the listening to the word of God, alive and resounding in the centuries and in the history of our individual souls, and in the mystical reality of the sacramental and propitiatory sacrifice of Christ.

Let us not say "new Mass" but rather "new epoch" in the life of the Church.

Interfaith Statement on Sex Education

Human sexuality is a gift of God, to be accepted with thanksgiving and used with reverence and joy. It is more than a mechanical instinct. Its many dimensions are intertwined with the total personality and character of the individual. Sex is a dynamic urge or power, arising from one's basic maleness or femaleness, and having complex physical, psychological and social dimensions. These dimensions, we affirm, must be shaped and guided by spiritual and moral considerations which derive from our Judeo-Christian heritage. The heritage teaches us that the source of values to guide human behavior is in God.

The sexual attitudes of children develop as part of their general social attitudes. Furthermore, respectful and considerate sexual attitudes help create healthy social attitudes. When the family and society view sex as loving and fulfilling, rather than prurient and exploitative, then both the social and sexual attitudes of children benefit. A healthful approach to sexual relations, willingness and ability to impart sexual information in a manner proportionate to the child's stage of development—these are among the elements which foster healthy sexual attitudes and behavior in the young. So, also, is resistance to social pressures which in some instances lead to premature sophistication or unhealthy attitudes in young people.

Responsibility for sex education belongs primarily to the child's parents or guardians. A home permeated by justice and love is the seedbed of sound sexual development among all family members. Both the attitudes and the activities of parents—toward each other and toward each child as an individual—affect this development. Health attitudes toward sex begin in the child's earliest years; they can best develop in an atmosphere that fosters in him a deep sense of his own self-worth, bolstered by love and understanding.

Sex education is not, however, only for the young; it is a life-long task whose aim is to help individuals develop their sexuality in a manner suited to their stage of life.

We recognize that some parents desire supplementary assistance from church or synagogue and from other agencies. Each community of faith should provide resources, leadership and opportunities as appropriate for its young people to learn about their development into manhood and womanhood, and for adults to grow in understanding of their roles as men and women in family and society in the light of their religious heritage.

In addition to parents and the religious community, the school and other community agencies can have a vital role in sex education in two particular ways:

1. They can integrate sound sexual information and attitudes with the total education which the child receives in social studies, civics, literature, history, home economics and the biological and behavioral sciences.

2. They can reach the large numbers of young people whose families have no religious identification but who need to understand their own sexuality and their role in society.

For those who would introduce sex education into the schools, however, the question of values and norms for sexual behavior is a problem—indeed, the most difficult problem. It is important that sex education not be reduced to the mere communication of information. Rather, this significant area of experience should be placed in a setting where rich human, personal and spiritual values can illuminate it and give it meaning. In such a setting, we are convinced it is not only possible but necessary to recognize certain basic moral principles, not as sectarian religious doctrine but as the moral heritage of Western civilization.

The challenge of resolving this problem of values in a pluralistic society makes it all the more imperative that communities planning to introduce sex education into the schools not only call upon educators to become involved in decisions about goals and techniques, but also invite parents and professionals in the community to take part in shaping such a curriculum.

To those groups responsible for developing school and community programs in sex education we suggest the following guidelines:

a) Such education should strive to create understanding and conviction that decisions about sexual behavior must be based on moral and ethical values, as well as on considerations of physical and emotional health, fear, pleasure, practical consequences, or concepts of personality development.

b) Such education must respect the cultural, familial and religious backgrounds and beliefs of individuals and must teach that the sexual development and behavior of each individual cannot take place in a vacuum but are instead related to the other aspects of his life and to his moral, ethical and religious codes.

c) It should point out how sex is distorted and exploited in our society and how this places heavy responsibility upon the individual, the family and institutions to cope in a constructive manner with the problem thus created.

d) It must recognize that in school sex education, insofar as it relates to moral and religious beliefs and values, complements the education conveyed through the family, the church or the synagogue. Sex education in the schools must proceed constructively, with understanding, tolerance and acceptance of difference.

e) It must stress the many points of harmony between moral values and beliefs about what is right and wrong that are held in common by the major religions on the one hand and generally accepted legal, social, psychological, medical and other values held in common by service professions and society generally.

f) Where strong differences of opinion exist on what is right and wrong sexual behavior, objective, informed and dignified discussion of both sides of such questions should be encouraged. However, in such cases, neither the sponsors of an educational program nor the teachers should attempt to give definite answers or to represent their personal moral and religious beliefs as the consensus of the major religions or of society generally.

g) Throughout such education human values and human dignity must be stressed as major bases for decisions of right and wrong; attitudes that build such respect should be encouraged as right, and those that tear down such respect should be condemned as wrong.

h) Such education should teach that sexuality is a part of the whole person and an aspect of his dignity as a human being.

i) It should teach that people who love each other try not to do anything that will harm each other.

j) It should teach that sexual intercourse within marriage offers the greatest possibility for personal fulfillment and social growth.

k) Finally, such a program of education must be based on sound content and must employ sound methods; it must be conducted by teachers and leaders qualified to do so by training and temperament.

The increased concern and interest in this vital area of human experience now manifested by parents, educators and religious leaders are cause for gratitude. We urge all to take a more active role—each in his own area of responsibility and competence—in promoting sound leadership and programs in sex education. We believe it possible to help our sons and daughters achieve a richer, fuller understanding of their sexuality, so that their children will enter a world where men and women live and work together in understanding, cooperation and love.

Religious Crises Among The Young

(Reprinted with permission by YOU, the Thomas More Association, 180 North Wabash Avenue, Chicago, Illinois)

What do conscientious parents do when their son or daughter suddenly declares for atheism? It may help, according to psychiatrist James A. Knight, to realize that this is not an uncommon experience. That does not, of course, mean that it is of no concern to the parents and that all they need to do is back away and, hoping for the best, let life go on. The adolescent's exploration of his religious convictions is indeed quite normal; his commitment, for a while at least, to atheism or agnosticism should not totally surprise his elders. With a better understanding of this phenomenon as a part of the religious development of personality, parents can avoid panic and can respond in a more constructive way.

Any maturing individual will reexamine the faith of his fathers. He must do this if he is to make it his own. From having accepted religious teachings and the rules of morality on the word of parents and others, a person must pass through the stage of looking at this religious heritage to see if he believes in it because of his own internal conviction. This is the process of internalizing the religious beliefs that are first accepted on external authority. No man achieves a mature religious outlook unless he enters into this stage of examining religious values in the light of his own motivation. To try to prevent this crisis of growth in a searching person is like staying the tides. To treat the individual who questions religious convictions as if he had done something wrong is equally unhelpful. Some of Dr. Knight's observations are quite helpful in understanding this phase of development and its implications for the relationship of parents with their questioning children.

During adolescence many young people "are not mature enough to distinguish between God and father," he writes. One of the growing person's tasks in adolescence is to separate God from father. This will involve him in struggles with authority for freedom and independence. "In order to clarify his confusion, and begin his movement toward independence," Dr. Knight observes, "he may reject God or father, or possibly both." It is after this painful but necessary step that he can work through his rebellion and arrive at a new understanding of and relationship to both God and his own father.

In reexamining the religion he has been taught, the young person frequently rebels against what he thought he was taught. He rejects, according to Dr. Knight, "his own childhood conceptions, for which he may illogically blame his culture, parents, and church. Many years may pass before he realizes that his rebellion was actually against his own immaturity."

Another source of doubt for the young as they examine religion is their confrontation with the problem of evil, of a whole world stewing in the juices of injustice and discord. This is deeply disturbing to their developing sensitivity for life and the values of love and relationship, whose values they are just beginning to appreciate. It is all incompatible with a Loving God, as they see it, and they may go on to reject Him or to decide that He is so distant that He has lost interest in human affairs. It is precisely characteristic of their humanitarian idealism at this stage to have to face the contradictions of the human condition and to reinspect the interpretations of life that were given them in early religious training.

It is not exactly surprising to find the most reflective of youth wondering why, if the older generation has accepted religion, they haven't practiced it better for their own sake and for the good of the rest of society. Formalized religious practice, with its institutionalized churches and rituals, also smacks of the same disappointing hypocrisy to young people. At this stage of growth, youth is witheringly critical and extraordinarily accurate in their indictment of the presumed failures of the older generation to do a better job in preserving and developing religious values. The turning off of old forms at this time may well be a sign of the depth of their desire for some religious vision of life which will not be disappointing in practice.

Dr. Knight also observes that during this period of inner struggle, social concerns become a major part of the young person's religion. Peace becomes the cause, and the religious figure who fights for social justice, the great ideal. Part of the psychological stirrings beneath all this rest on the adolescent's "search for peace within himself." He is engaged in a struggle for growth, confronting the contradictory faces of reality, and attempting to put together some sustaining philosophy of life. Dr. Knight suggests that the adolescent has a need at this time for "the steadying influence of moral strength and unity" and a "stable environment" which go a long way in meeting the emotional needs of conflict-ridden youngsters. It is at this point that he is in need of contact with elders who have achieved a mature religious outlook and with an institutional Church which understands and responds to, rather than aggravates, his needs.

The young man or woman is just warming at this time to an understanding of the meaning of love. Never will he be more idealistic about its possibilities or more disillusioned by an older generation that has given up or compromised their own struggle to love. The problem of integrating the sexual aspects of love with an understanding of the broader picture of human and divine love is urgent at this time. In other words, the young person is dealing with what is most precious in life, is searching for a stable and less than hypocritical standard of belief to guide him, and quickly turns away from those who cannot bring much understanding to him during this period.

The avowed agnostic may indeed be a person in the middle of one or the other of these aspects of growth. He will not be helped much by those who can only back away from him or condemn him for his treachery against an ancient religious cause. Neither is the answer in a reinforced dogmatism, which to him sounds like the religion of his child-hood repeated in a louder and more unforgiving voice.

It is clear that youth needs understanding from people who are strong enough in their own religious convictions to share the struggle of searching and growing with them. The problem is not unusual nor unfortunate. What is unfortu-nate is the presence of too many older people who have never seriously reexamined their own religious convictions and who can only respond with some musty fundamentalism, or who are so faint-hearted at every challenge of youth that they meekly back away without revealing their own values to them.

Eugene Kennedy

APPENDIX IV

A Selected Bibliography

Listed here is a select bibliography which will help the Middle Catholic in his self-education. The list is personal and opinionated. The first six books are helpful and non-technical. The rest are all good and I have listed them alphabetically by author.

Killgallon and Weber, *Beyond the Commandments,* Herder and Herder, New York, 1964. Anything these two Chicago priests write individually or together is worth while. They have done as much as anyone to interpret Vatican II to the public. This book is as good an insight into morality and sin as any. It gives a good understanding to new approaches.

Reedy and Andrews, *The Perplexed Catholic,* Ave Maria Press, Notre Dame, Indiana, 1968. Both of these men are considered liberals but they are both humane and understanding. Father Reedy especially deserves some kind of a medal for keeping his balance concerning renewal.

Eugene Kennedy, *The People Are the Church,* Doubleday and Company, Inc., Garden City, N.Y., 1969. Father Kennedy is a liberal also and an investigator into the need and means of renewal. This book summarized a good case for the need.

Gerard Sloyan, *Worship in a New Key,* The Liturgical Conference, Herder and Herder, New York, 1965. Father Sloyan is a genuine scholar with wit and insight. Anything he writes is worth reading. This is a basic book on liturgy.

John Tracy Ellis, *American Catholicism,* University of Chicago Press, 1955. This slim volume is still one of the best summaries on the early Church in America. Msgr. Ellis is a scholar and writes well.

Andrew Greeley, *The Hesitant Pilgrim,* Sheed and Ward,

218

New York, 1966. Father Greeley is the patron saint of renewal explanation. His output is prodigious. He is beginning to sound like himself, but the quality of his writings
has been consistently high. This is a fine book on renewal.
Any of his other books are worth reading.

OTHER BOOKS OF BACKGROUND

Baum, Gregory, *The Credibility of the Church Today*,
Herder and Herder, New York, 1968. This is Father Baum's
reply to Charles Davis, the famed English priest-theologian
who left the Church. This book requires some background,
but it is worth reading.

Bausch, William, *It Is The Lord!*, Fides Publishers, Inc.,
Notre Dame, Indiana, 1970. My own book so this recom-
mendation is biased. This is a book summarizing the new
looks at sin, morality and new approaches to confession.

Bertocci, Peter, *Sex, Love and The Person*, Sheed and
Ward, New York, 1967. A personalist's view to traditional
morality. The first chapters are not easy reading, but it's
worth the effort.

Borromeo, Charles Sister M., *The New Nuns*, The New
American Library, 1967. Sister has edited several good
pieces on what nuns are thinking.

Callahan, Daniel, *The New Church: Essays in Catholic
Reform*, Charles Scribner's Sons, New York, 1966. Dan
Callahan is always worth reading even when one disagrees
with him. He is one of the few scholars who is willing to
admit that he, too, is a pilgrim and can and does change his
mind on renewal. He's willing to grow and to explore.

Campbell, Robert, *Spectrum of Catholic Attitudes*, Bruce
Publishing Co., Milwaukee, 1969. Father Campbell has edited a series of comments by various laymen on renewal
who represent the spectrum from liberal to conservative.
Interesting.

Champlin, Joseph M., *"Don't You Really Love Me?"*, Ave
Maria Press, Notre Dame, Indiana, 1968. Written in a
straight forward way this is a fine case for youthful premarital chastity. Some adults may be upset by its bluntness,
but it is very well thought of by the adolescents themselves.

Curran, Charles, *Contraception: Authority and Dissent*, Herder and Herder, New York, 1969. Father Curran has edited the pros and cons on this subject.

Dolan, John P., *History of The Reformation*, Desclee, New York, 1964. A little heavy-handed treatment of the Reformation, but never dull.

Gleason, Robert, S.J., *The Restless Religious*, Pflaum Press, Dayton, Ohio, 1968. A good look at the topic.

Greeley, Andrew, *Life For A Wanderer*, Doubleday and Company, Inc., Garden City, N.Y., 1969. Good book on modern spirituality.

Guitton, Jean, *Great Heresies and Church Councils*, Harper and Row, New York, 1965. The famed Frenchman's valuable history.

Hoyt, Robert G., *Issues That Divide The Church*, The Macmillan Company, New York, 1967. An interesting paperback edited by Mr. Hoyt giving several notable people's view of today's major church issues.

Kennedy, Eugene, *Fashion Me A People*, Sheed and Ward, New York, 1967. Good Kennedy on renewal.

Kung, Hans, *The Church*, Burns and Oates, London, 1968. Father Kung is one of the pioneers of renewal. His book is well done and insightful.

McBrien, Richard, *Do We Need The Church?*, Harper and Row, New York, 1969. Don't let the title throw you off. An original and stimulating book; requires some background.

McGoey, John H., S.F.M., *The Sins Of The Just*, Bruce Publishing Company, Milwaukee, 1963. Readable and even entertaining writing on some basic flaws in convent life.

McKenzie, John L., *The Roman Catholic Church*, Holt, Rinehart and Winston, New York. 1969. Father McKenzie's view of the Church. Interesting and provocative.

A New Catechism, Herder and Herder, New York, 1967. The famous Dutch catechism giving all of the new slants on one's approach to God.

Pelikan, Jaroslav, *The Riddle of Roman Catholicism*, Abingdon Press, New York, 1959. This is a good book to read because it gives an insight to a friendly Protestant's view of the Church before Vatican II.

Peter, Laurence J., and Hull, Raymond, *The Peter Principle*, William Marrow and Company, Inc., New York, 1969. This nonreligious book is so delightful and so applicable to some Church problems that it is worth reading, as is *Parkinson's Law* for the same reason.

Powers, J. F., *Morte D'Urban*, Doubleday and Company, Inc., Garden City, New York, 1956. A novelist's entertaining and accurate view of the humanity of the priest.

Quoist, Michael, *Prayers*, Sheed and Ward, New York, 1963. An example of the new free flowing style of praying in a contemporary way.

Rynne, Xavier, *Vatican Council II*, Farrar, Strauss and Giroux, New York, 1968. A one-sided but highly readable account of what went on at the Vatican Council.

Sheed, Frank, *Is It The Same Church?*, Sheed and Ward, London and Sydney, 1968. Mr. Sheed is always readable. He is deep and witty. One of the great layman of the age.

Sloyan, Gerard, *How Do I Know I'm Doing Right?*, Pflaum Press, Dayton, Ohio, 1966. Father Sloyan at his best on morality.

Thorman, Donald J., *American Catholics Face The Future*, Dimension Books, Inc., Wilkes-Barre, Pa., 1968. Mr. Thorman is the author of the pioneer book *The Emerging Layman*. The present book is a discussion of renewal from the layman's point of view.

Trevor, Meriol, *Prophets and Guardians*, Doubleday and Company, Inc., Garden City, New York, 1969. This book covers the beginning of the twentieth century and the furor over Modernism. It is interesting because it sheds a lot of light on origins of the problems that have arisen since Vatican II.

Winkler, Brother Julius, F.S.C., *A Generation Apart.* A Christian Brothers Publication, St. Mary's College Press, Winona, Minnesota, 1969. Brother Winkler has edited one of the best compilations on youth I've seen. Worth reading to keep in touch.